Testimonials

 W9-BTZ-771

"This is great! I was surprised to find out how easy it really is to improve my listening ability. This book has made a real difference for me. I'm glad I found it."

Kathy Patton
ABF Freight Systems, Inc.
Sales Representative

"Everyone I know could get something out of this book. It ought to be required reading."

Mark Towers
Professional Speaker and Consultant
Towers Consulting

"I thought I was a good listener. But when I started looking through it, I found a lot of things I hadn't realized. I learned a lot from it. My employees will too."

Diane MacPherson
Customer Service Manager
National Seminars Group

"This should be required reading. Good communication is essential for good business. *Learn to Listen* will most definitely get you on your way."

Gary N. Beatty
Mid-Central/Sysco
Manager-Contract & Design

Learn
to
Listen

Written by
Jim Dugger

National Press Publications
A Division of Rockhurst College Continuing Education Center, Inc.
6901 West 63rd Street • P.O. Box 2949 • Shawnee Mission, KS 66201-1349
1-800-258-7246 • (913) 432-7757

Learn to Listen
Published by National Press Publications
© 1992 National Press Publications
A Division of Rockhurst College Continuing Education Center, Inc.

Printed in the United States of America.

 2 3 4 5 6 7 8 9 10

ISBN #1-55852-084-8

About Rockhurst College Continuing Education Center, Inc.

Rockhurst College Continuing Education Center, Inc., is committed to providing lifelong learning opportunities through the integration of innovative education and training.

National Seminars Group, a division of Rockhurst College Continuing Education Center, Inc., has its finger on the pulse of America's business community. We've trained more than 2 million people in every imaginable occupation to be more productive and advance their careers. Along the way, we've learned a few things. Like what it takes to be successful ... how to build the skills to make it happen ... and how to translate learning into results. Millions of people from thousands of companies around the world turn to National Seminars for training solutions.

National Press Publications is our product and publishing division. We offer a complete line of the finest self-study and continuing-learning resources available anywhere. These products present our industry-acclaimed curriculum and training expertise in a concise, action-oriented format you can put to work right away. Packed with real-world strategies and hands-on techniques, these resources are guaranteed to help you meet the career and personal challenges you face every day.

INTRODUCTION

Learn to Listen Was Created with You, the Business User, in Mind

Written in a no-nonsense style, this book introduces ideas, gives examples and offers opportunities for examining your listening skills and habits. Key concepts are highlighted, steps are outlined and definitions are presented.

No matter what listening skill level you have achieved, you will learn to improve in areas such as:

- Active listening

- Nonverbal communication

- Effective listening techniques

- Reflective listening

- Helping poor listeners listen to you

- Minimizing conflict

In this book you will also identify:

- The four types of listening

- The five steps of active listening

- Ways to monitor nonverbal communication and filters

- Ways to separate your personal and professional lives

- Long-term filters

- Techniques to control barriers

- Three key steps to reflective listening

- Three principles for responding without judgment

- Listening techniques for conflicts

- Personal communication pitfalls and patterns

- Four guidelines to better listening with family and friends

- How to listen to yourself!

To get the maximum benefit from this book as a self-study course, answer the questions and complete the exercises. They were all designed to pinpoint your strengths and weaknesses and help you objectively examine your listening habits.

You can use this book also as a quick-reference manual to look up listening techniques as needed — for both personal and professional situations.

F OREWORD

A Book on Listening?

You bet!

You may think that you are listening all the time — that you have listened, in fact, for as long as you can remember.

You have listened to your parents. You have listened to your friends. You have listened to your teachers, to your co-workers, to your bosses and to your clients. You have listened to your spouse or your significant other and to your children.

The list is endless.

Have you really listened, though, or do you actually only *hear* these people? And, if you have listened, have you done so actively and with an open mind? Do you realize there really is a difference between truly listening to and merely hearing the messages others want to share with you?

Most likely you have done a little of both — hearing and listening — at one time or another. And, that is natural. This book, however, will help you to *listen* more often and with greater skill. Yes, listening can — and should — be thought of and developed as a skill. It is never too late to perfect this skill, and even very good listeners can become better at it.

The key is learning to practice Active Listening. The active listener has learned how to overcome the filters and barriers to effective communication. Once you overcome these obstacles and become a more proficient, active listener, you will notice improvements in your relationships with family, co-workers, friends ... you get the picture.

That's why this book about listening was created.

Sheryl Kudy
Editor
National Press Publications

CONTENTS

Contents

CHAPTER 1

Overview

Listening is one of the most important skills you can possess.
However, it is one of the skills that is seldom taught in school. At
best, schools "talk" about listening, but very few actually teach it.
What listening skills you have learned have been by trial and error.
You have learned that just because you hear something doesn't
mean you listened. Hearing is a physical act. Listening is an
emotional and intellectual act. Hearing acknowledges sounds;
listening requires that you understand what was said.

> **Listening is the emotional and intellectual act of hearing
> what is communicated and responding to both the verbal
> and nonverbal message being sent.**

Checklist: Why Should I Want to Listen Better?

Directions: **Place a check in each box that indicates why you want to listen better.**

I want to:

☐   improve communication.

☐   be in control of the situation.

☐   lessen arguments.

☐   show that I care.

☐   better understand my world.

☐   improve my memory.

☐   be a better manager.

☐   be a better employee.

☐   be a better spouse.

☐   be a better parent.

☐   be a better friend.

Now, take a look at what you have checked. Each of these areas is covered in this book. To become a better listener you need to know just two rules.

> **Two Rules for Improving Your Listening Skills**
>
> 1. **Learn how to use Active Listening.**
> 2. **Practice Active Listening skills.**

What Is Active Listening?

It Involves Several Steps:

- Demonstrating empathy for the speaker. When you show that you value what the speaker is saying, you demonstrate empathy.

- Being nonjudgmental of the speaker. When you do not criticize or put down the speaker's ideas, even though you don't agree, you are being nonjudgmental.

- Understanding nonverbal communication and how it affects your perception of what's being said. Nonverbal communication includes everything from eye contact to gestures to the way something is said.

- Understanding the emotional filters that affect your understanding of what is being said. Emotional filters are emotions that get in the way of you hearing what is being said. They produce mental blocks.

- Being prepared to listen. By having a knowledge of your own filters and nonverbal communication, you are better prepared to understand how they affect you and those you are listening to.

- Being motivated to listen. If you are not motivated to listen, the words "will go in one ear and out the other."

- Striving for accuracy. Not only is it important to listen but it is also important to listen carefully and accurately.

**C
A
S
E

S
T
U
D
Y**

Case Study:

Max stops by your desk at the office and flops himself into the chair. He looks nervously left and right before he starts to speak. He speaks quickly with a slight slur, almost as if he's been drinking. You think you smell alcohol, but then it might be Max's cologne. "Can you believe what old man Smith just did?" Max looks over his shoulder. "I can't believe he's on my case again. He said that this was the last time. Either I shape up or ship out." With the last statement, Max looks distraught. "I gotta have this job. Me and Marge can't make it on one income. We're overextended." He fiddles nervously with the paperweight on your desk, then starts to get up, looking once more to see if the hall is clear. "Gee, thanks for listening, Terry," and he leaves.

Case Study Questions:

1. What was the content that was communicated?

2. What was the intent of the speaker?

3. What was communicated nonverbally?

4. How did I react nonverbally to what was being said?

5. What in my background or personality got in the way of what was being communicated?

6. Was I empathic toward the speaker?

7. Did I respond without judging the speaker?

Five Steps to Active Listening

1. **Listen to the content.** Listen to what the speaker is saying in terms of facts and ideas. Listen to his words rather than just his nonverbal communication. Be as accurate as you can. Use your intellect to hear what he says. Ideas that are far-fetched can be delivered in such a way that the audience will accept them. Be aware of what the speaker is saying.

2. **Listen to the intent.** Listen to the emotional meaning of the speaker and what he is saying. Use your intuition to "hear" the underlying messages. The speaker may use various methods of delivery, such as persuasion, to get you to agree with him. His intent may be, for example, to convince the audience that the opposition's point of view is wrong. He may do this by "damning by faint praise." In other words, he slants his delivery to sound as if he is praising the opposition when, in fact, he is tearing it down.

3. **Assess the speaker's nonverbal communication.** Read and interpret what the speaker is "saying" with his body language and other nonverbal signals. Be aware of nonverbals such as gestures or posture. The speaker will communicate more with this than with verbal communication. Nonverbal signals also include eye contact, tone of voice and facial expression.

4. **Monitor your nonverbal communication and emotional filters.** Be aware of the messages you are sending with your nonverbal communication. Be aware of emotional filters that affect your understanding of the receiver. Emotional filters are those "hot buttons" that cause you to stop listening. Words such as "layoffs" or "foreign investor" may cause you to see red. If you are aware of your emotional filters, you can control them.

5. **Listen to the speaker with empathy and without judgment.** Try to put yourself in the speaker's shoes and understand what is shaping his feelings. Don't prejudge the speaker. Listening with empathy and without judgment tells the speaker that you understand what he is saying. It validates the speaker. You may not agree with what he is saying, but it shows that you will take the time to listen to his message.

> *"The most important thing in communication is to hear what isn't being said."*
>
> *John W. Roper*

Active Listening requires your complete attention to the speaker.

Case Study:

Dirk, Donna, Mary and Bill are all middle managers at Bartons, Inc., a company specializing in children's clothes. Listen in as they start a meeting to discuss sales.

"Good morning, folks," says Dirk as he joins the others. As usual he is 10 minutes late. They nod good morning, showing disapproval on their faces. "I've got the report from Thomas and Sons concerning its shipment."

"Donna, would you pass me the report from Calhoun's Department Stores?" asks Mary, ignoring Dirk.

"Sure, it's quite interesting. You were saying, Dirk?"

"I've got the report from Thomas and Sons on its last shipment."

"Oh, Thomas and Sons," replies Mary, "that's my old account. Let me see it."

"They really burn me up, dropping our toddler's line for Smithton's. I worked long and hard on that account." Dirk's face gets redder. "I put in lots of time on it."

"This is interesting," answers Mary. Donna sips her coffee and looks out the window.

"I hear you saying that you feel like you've been cheated on this one," responds Bill.

"You've hit the nail on the head! Now I've got to go back out and resell them."

"How do you feel about that?" asks Bill.

"Oh, I guess I can do it. I've done it before. Thanks for listening to me blow off steam, Bill."

"Sure, any time."

"Did you see Thomas and Sons dropped your toddler line, Dirk?" asks Mary.

"Dirk's got a new toddler line?" replies Donna, coming up from her daydream.

Each of the people in the case study is using a type of listening. After reading the following definitions, answer the questions about the case study.

Four Types of Listening

- **Inactive Listening** — This is the kind of listening you want to avoid. It is inefficient and unproductive. You hear only the words. They go in one ear and out the other.

- **Selective Listening** — This kind of listening is probably the most common. It is when you hear only what you want to hear. You filter the message. Like Inactive Listening, it is also inefficient and unproductive.

- **Active Listening** — This is when you make a conscious effort not only to hear the words but also to listen for the complete message the speaker is sending. It takes into consideration the intent and the nonverbal communication of the speaker. Active Listening also uses empathy and is nonjudgmental.

- **Reflective Listening** — Like Active Listening, Reflective Listening takes in the whole message. It is particularly important if you are dealing with a complicated issue or resolving a conflict. Reflective Listening is used to clarify what is being said and to convey mutual understanding. The listener often asks the speaker questions to help clarify the message.

> *"Teach me half the gladness*
> *That thy brain must know,*
> *Such harmonious madness*
> *From my lips would flow,*
> *The world should listen then, as I am*
> *listening now."*
>
> **Percy Bysshe Shelley**

Case Study Questions:

1. Which type of listening is Donna using?

2. Which type of listening is Mary using?

3. Which type of listening is Bill using?

Analysis of the Case Study:

Donna is using Inactive Listening. She hears what the others are saying but blocks their meaning. She is concerned more with her coffee and daydreams than anything else.

Mary is using Selective Listening. She is interested only when Dirk mentions Thomas and Sons, her old account. She does not, however, continue to listen to what Dirk is saying. Instead she reads the report.

Bill is listening both actively and reflectively to Dirk. He takes into consideration the content, intent and nonverbal messages Dirk is sending. He then responds to Dirk in a nonthreatening manner, simply reflecting back in different words what Dirk has just said. Note that Bill gave Dirk no advice, nor did he argue with him. He simply acted genuinely interested in what Dirk had to say. Dirk then thanked Bill for being a good listener.

> **Active and Reflective Listening**
> **are the marks of a good listener.**

Listening Inventory

The following is a listening inventory to see if you are presently practicing Active Listening. After reading each question, give yourself a score of one to five. When you finish taking the inventory, add up your score and check it against the inventory scale. The letters after the questions are keyed to areas you may need to work on.

Question	Never	Sometimes			Always
	1	2	3	4	5
1. Do you find yourself understanding what was said but not what was meant? (A)					
2. Do you find it hard to concentrate on what the speaker is saying because of external distractions, such as noise or movement? (B)					
3. Do you find it hard to concentrate on what the speaker is saying because of internal distractions, such as worry, fear, being unprepared or daydreaming? (A)					
4. Do you find yourself responding to what the speaker implies rather than what he says? (A)					
5. Do you find yourself responding in anger to words, stated or implied, that for all logical reasons should not make you angry? (A)					
6. Do you have trouble reading a person's body language? (D)					
7. Do you find it difficult to respond to a speaker in a nonjudgmental way if you don't agree with him? (E)					
8. Do you find it difficult to respond to a speaker in a nonjudgmental way if you don't like him? (E)					
9. Do you find yourself preparing your response before the speaker has finished? (F)					
10. Do you find yourself listening selectively, hearing only those words and ideas that you want to hear? (A)					
11. Are there certain words, phrases or actions that consistently trigger certain positive or negative responses in you? (F)					
12. Do you find yourself asking, "What did you say?" even though you've heard the speaker? (B,C)					
13. Do you rely on others to interpret what happened at a meeting? (A)					

Now check your totals against the Listening Inventory Scale below.

13-20: You are a very good listener.
21-32: You are a fairly good listener.
33-45: You are an average listener.
46-58: You are a fairly poor listener.
59-65: You are a poor listener.

These questions relate to issues covered in this book, and they should help you pinpoint some of your strengths and weaknesses in listening. Take a look at your responses in the listening inventory. Do they follow a particular pattern? The questions are keyed so you can easily identify the areas you need to work on.

Listening Inventory Key

A — Emotional Filters

B — Physical Distractions

C — Internal Distractions

D — Body Language

E — Nonjudgmental Responses

F — Filters/Prejudging

Summary

Almost everyone wants to improve his or her listening. This workbook will help you do that. In the following chapters, you will find tips on using Active Listening in the workplace, common barriers that get in the way of listening, emotional and mental filters that get in the way of communication, how to use reflective listening and how to get someone who is a poor listener to listen to you more carefully. If you put these techniques into practice, you may receive the ultimate compliment: "You're a good listener."

Active Listening

In Chapter 1 you took a listening inventory designed to identify your strengths and weaknesses when listening.

Directions: Transfer the number of times you checked a column from the listening inventory to the following chart. For example, if you put a check in box 2 for the first question on the listening inventory, place a check mark in box 2 for the first question.

Question	Never		Sometimes		Always
	1	2	3	4	5
1. (A)					
2. (B)					
3. (A)					
4. (A)					
5. (A)					
6. (D)					
7. (E)					
8. (E)					
9 . (F)					
10. (A)					
11. (F)					
12. (B, C)					
13. (A)					

Now add up the scores for each letter. For example, A in Question 1 will be worth 2 points if you checked column 2 or will be worth 4 if you checked column 4, and so on. Circle your score on the following continuum for each letter. If your score falls in a box, you need to work on that area.

Listening Inventory Key

A — Emotional Filters   6 — 12 — 18 — | 24 — 30 |

B — Physical Distractions   2 — 4 — 6 — | 8 — 10 |

C — Internal Distractions   1 — 2 — 3 — | 4 — 5 |

D — Body Language   1 — 2 — 3 — | 4 — 5 |

E — Nonjudgmental Responses   2 — 4 — 6 — | 8 — 10 |

F — Filters/Prejudging   2 — 4 — 6 — | 8 — 10 |

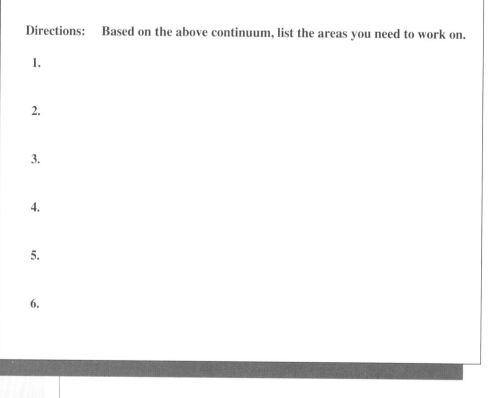

Areas I Need to Work on

Directions: Based on the above continuum, list the areas you need to work on.

1.

2.

3.

4.

5.

6.

> ## The goal of all good listening is to tune in to the speaker.

By teaching you what to concentrate on, this book will help you to improve your listening skills even more. One way is to practice Active Listening.

Active Listening

Active Listening is a method of improving your listening skills so you can be effective in your business and personal life. There are five steps in Active Listening. Look at each of the five steps in relationship to your own listening inventory.

The Five Steps of Active Listening

- Listen to the content.
- Listen to the intent.
- Assess the speaker's nonverbal communication.
- Monitor your nonverbal communication and filters.
- Listen to the speaker with empathy and without judgment.

- **Listen to the Content**

Definition:

Content is the words of the speaker and the facts, figures, ideas and logic the words convey.

Example:

Leslie gets up to speak at her weekly department meeting. She is nervous and fidgety. She looks a little flushed. She says, "I have just received word that this department will be experiencing a 25-percent cutback effective in two months. It will be my responsibility to decide how we will cut back. I know now that I can pare the budget by only 10 percent and still maintain services that we now have. I anticipate that we will have to cut one to one-and-a-half positions. Those people may be transferred rather than laid off." She opens up the meeting for discussion and questions. From the way she acts, it is obvious that this is not a decision she wants to make.

> *"To take what there is and use it, without waiting forever in vain for the preconceived — to dig deep into the actual and get something out of that — this doubtless is the right way to live."*
>
> **Henry James**

13

Example Questions:

1. Who will make the cuts?

2. How many positions may be cut?

3. Will the people cut be laid off?

4. What percentage must be cut?

Example Analysis:

The content is only the words that Leslie used. Her nonverbal communication shows that she is uncomfortable dealing with the information. An Active Listener will listen to the content and assess the nonverbals also. If you are not actively listening, you may hear the term "cutback" and block out the rest of the content because you are thinking about how you will be affected by the cutbacks.

Key Idea:

Only 10 percent of what is communicated in a business setting is expressed in words. Those words are the core or the content of the message. If you do not understand the content that is being communicated, ask for clarification.

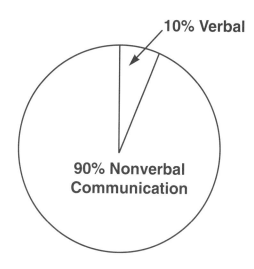

10% Verbal

90% Nonverbal Communication

- **Listen to the Intent**

Definition:

The intent of the message is a balance between the content, the nonverbal communication, the speaker's background and whatever bias or position the speaker may have regarding the subject.

Example Analysis:

In the previous example about cutbacks, it was Leslie's intent to tell her department about the cutbacks, but at the same time her nonverbal communication indicated she was not comfortable having to make the decision.

Key Idea:

The better you know the speaker, the more you will understand his intent.

Questions to Ask When Assessing Intent:

1. What is the speaker's track record on the issue being presented?

2. Does the speaker usually try to impress the boss?

3. Is the speaker in line for a promotion or retirement?

4. Is the speaker easygoing, hard to get along with or neutral?

5. Does the speaker's background bias what is being said?

6. Does the speaker's nonverbal language bias what is being said?

When you are listening for the intent of a speaker, you are listening to "why" he says something rather than "what" he says.

Key Idea:

Use your intuition to "hear" the intent. Use your intellect to "hear" the content. Do not use your emotions to interpret the intent. Use your intellect for that.

Intellectually, you could see that Leslie was uncomfortable. Intuitively, you could sense that also. If you use your emotions to interpret the intent, you might go overboard and feel sorry for Leslie because she is so uncomfortable. This in turn could cloud your hearing of what she is saying. Intellectually, you can empathize with her dilemma. You need to keep a clear head so that you listen to how the cutbacks are going to affect you.

• **Assess the Speaker's Nonverbal Communication**

Definition:

Nonverbal communication is a combination of body language and tone of voice. Verbal communication deals only with the words that are spoken. How words are spoken or the tone of voice used is considered nonverbal communication. In the example about Leslie, the way she delivered her message, her flushed face and her nervousness were all nonverbal signals sending a message.

Communication

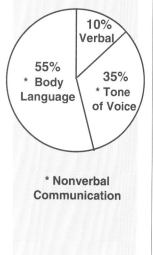

* Nonverbal
Communication

> **Fifty-five percent of nonverbal communication is body language. Thirty-five percent of nonverbal communication is the tone of voice used.**

When you practice Active Listening, you are "listening" to the speaker's body language as well as his actual words. Nonverbal communication deals with "how" something is said and delivered rather than "what" is said.

There are three channels of communication used in Active Listening; two of these are nonverbal:

- Verbal
- Visual
- Tactile (Kinesthetic)

These three channels are used in conjunction with each other. Seldom will you find one used exclusively.

How to Assess the Speaker's Nonverbal Communication

Directions: Observe a communication situation such as a television news show, talk show or situation comedy for a short period of time. Record what is being communicated below:

Content

- **Verbal (words only)**

    "I told them that I wasn't interested in renewing my contract with NBC."

Intent

- **Verbal (tone of voice)**

    The above was said sarcastically.

- **Visual (nonverbal communication)**

    - **Posture**

        The interviewee was hunched forward.

    - **Eye contact**

        The interviewee had no eye contact with the host.

    - **Motion**

        The interviewee seemed agitated.

- **Touch (tactile communication)**

    The host reached over and touched the arm of the interviewee as if to calm him.

Analysis of What Was Communicated

Directions: Complete the following questions based on the observations you have recorded on the previous page.

1. Was the content different from the intent? In what way?

2. Were the speaker's biases evident? What were they?

3. How did the speaker's nonverbals change the meaning of the content?

4. Did the listener pick up on the nonverbal communication?

5. How could the speaker have been more effective with either his verbal or nonverbal communication?

• **Monitor Your Nonverbal Communications and Filters**

Definition:

Filters are ways of responding to information, ideas, words and even nonverbal communication that you have developed during your lifetime.

Example:

If you grew up in a rural community where hard work was expected and a person's word was good for sealing a contract, you may have trouble listening to someone who talks about how lazy his co-workers are or how you can't trust anyone. Your filters will have trouble believing him. These expectations that affect your listening ability are explored further in Chapter 3.

Key Idea:

Each person filters information through his biases, experiences and expectations and responds accordingly. You cannot eliminate your emotional filters. You can control them by practicing Active Listening.

There are many possible biases, expectations and experiences you may have. They include:

Biases

- A bias for or against upper management
- A bias for or against middle management
- A bias for or against blue-collar workers
- A bias for or against men
- A bias for or against women
- A bias for or against a particular political party
- A bias for or against a particular worker
- A bias for or against a particular race
- A bias for or against a particular religion
- A bias for or against a particular age group

Expectations

- Higher or lower expectations depending on your biases

Experiences

- No experience with the situation the person is talking about
- A positive or a negative experience with the situation the person is talking about

"Men's thoughts are much according to their inclination ... and infused opinions."

Francis Bacon

Reaction Worksheet

Directions: Write a brief reaction to each of the following statements:

- "We need to eliminate 40 percent of the workforce because of the economy."

- "Sales are up 13 percent and are projected to rise another 5 percent during the second quarter."

- "The federal government just announced an increase in corporate taxes and a decrease in personal income tax."

- "You are being transferred to another state to develop a new territory."

Reaction Worksheet

Directions: Now write a reaction to the statements given on page 20 as you think the following people would react.

- **Your immediate supervisor**

- **Your subordinate**

- **The president of the company**

- **Your parents**

- **Your spouse or significant other**

- **Your teenager**

- **Your neighbor**

Note: The words stayed the same. Only the filters changed.

• **Listen to the Speaker with Empathy and Without Judgment**

Definition:

Empathy means that you accept the speaker and accept his communication as worthwhile. Listening in a nonjudgmental way means that you listen with an open mind and don't prejudge. You do not have to accept the speaker's ideas or points of view.

Example:

Kyle, your manager, says to you, "I'm having trouble in the Kokomo office. I think one of the managers is stealing us blind. I want you to go there and do some investigating and see what's going on." You have heard from some reliable sources that the problem is really with Kyle and the way he is managing. If you are listening with empathy and without judgment, you will validate what he is saying and not judge its truth or merit. You may choose to ask him questions to further clarify the situation.

Example Questions:

1. What emotional or mental filters could get in the way of your hearing what Kyle was saying?

2. What question might you ask Kyle to clarify why he thinks the Kokomo office is stealing?

Key Idea:

Empathic and nonjudgmental listening sends the message to the speaker that you care about him and what he is communicating. All other steps of Active Listening are useless unless you listen with empathy and without judging the speaker.

"The word 'listen' contains the same letters as the word 'silent'."

Alfred Bandel

For many, listening with empathy is not difficult. It comes naturally. Empathy tells the speaker that you accept him. For others, empathy is extremely difficult because of preconceived notions about the speaker or the topic. Listening in a nonjudgmental way goes hand in hand with listening with empathy. When you listen without passing an opinion, you suspend your judgment of the speaker and what he says.

Our emotional and mental filters protect us from what is uncomfortable or what does not fit into our set of values. This makes Active Listening difficult because we must constantly fight against the tendency not to hear the unpleasant. You must tell yourself, "I will not fill in the gaps of the speaker with my ideas, thoughts, biases and opinions. I will resist the desire to make judgments."

To accomplish Active Listening, practice the 12 effective listening techniques on the following page.

One person's exuberance is the next person's annoyance.

12 Effective Listening Techniques

1. Eliminate as many external distractions as you can, such as by closing your door or not answering the phone.

2. Eliminate as many internal distractions as you can by controlling your emotions.

3. Come to meetings prepared so that you can actively listen to others. Look over the agenda. Jot down ideas and points you want to cover. Do your homework on the topics to be discussed.

4. Take notes if you begin to daydream.

5. Do not respond only to what the speaker implies. Respond to the total communication: content, intent and nonverbal communication.

6. Identify words that trigger your anger and then control your reaction. Try to understand why these words make you instantly angry. If you see red when someone says, "Robotics are the future," you will not be able to think and listen clearly.

7. Respond to a speaker without judging what he or she says.

8. Do not prepare your response while someone is still talking.

9. Do not go into a communication situation with your mind already made up. If you go into a meeting with your mind made up, you may miss an important point that could change your mind.

10. Negotiate behavior with yourself. Understand ahead of time what your options may be to certain words or ideas expressed. This is not prejudging, this is preparing.

11. If you realize you are not listening, physically move forward in your seat. If standing, move toward the speaker if possible.

12. Do not rely on others to interpret what happened in a meeting or what was said. If you rely on others to interpret, you will get your information secondhand and filtered through their emotional and mental filters.

Action Steps to Accomplish the 12 Effective Listening Techniques

Listed below are the techniques that you can use immediately to start practicing Active Listening. Each of these will be further developed later in this book.

> **Effective Listening Technique #1:**
> **Eliminate as many external**
> **distractions as you can.**

Action Step to Accomplish This Technique

Directions: List five external distractions such as noise or movement in your workplace that you can control.

Example: *Telephone calls constantly interrupt me.*

1.

2.

3.

4.

5.

**Effective Listening Technique #2:
Eliminate as many internal
distractions as you can.**

Action Step to Accomplish This Technique

Directions: List five internal distractions you must deal with.

Example: *I worry about my son's driving record.*

1.

2.

3.

4.

5.

> **Effective Listening Technique #3:**
> **Come to meetings prepared so**
> **that you can actively listen to the others.**

To accomplish this technique, follow these steps:

- Have materials organized before the meeting so you don't have to fumble around for them while someone refers to them.

- Have writing materials at hand.

- Control as many external distractions as you can, such as closing the door to outside noises, sitting in a listening-advantage position, closing the blinds to distracting views and turning off noise makers such as radios, intercoms and phones.

- Control as many internal distractions as possible. Promise yourself you will deal with a problem that is bothering you after the meeting instead of during the meeting. Anticipate how the meeting will go so that you can listen instead of react.

> **Effective Listening Technique #4:**
> **Take notes if you begin to daydream.**

Here are a couple of action steps to accomplish this technique:

- Have paper and pencil ready to take notes.

- Get into the habit of note-taking by tuning in to both the content and intent of the speaker.

"The beginning is the most important part of the work."

Plato

> **Effective Listening Technique #5:**
> **Do not respond only to what the speaker implies.**
> **Respond to the total communication:**
> **content, intent and nonverbal communication.**

Follow this action step to accomplish this technique:

- Set up your note-taking using the following format until it becomes automatic. Until you subconsciously can assess the content, intent and nonverbal communication of a speaker, the following format will be helpful.

Speaker	Content	Intent	Nonverbal
Example: *Roger*	**Example:** *Christmas bonus*	**Example:** *Show goodwill*	**Example:** *Acted like Scrooge*

Effective Listening Technique #6:
Identify words that trigger your anger and then control
your reaction. Try to understand why these words
make you instantly angry.

Action Step to Accomplish This Technique

Directions: List words that make you see red. Then analyze why they affect you that way.

Words That Trigger My Anger	Why These Words Anger Me
Management by Objectives	*Supervisor rammed it down our throats*

> **Effective Listening Technique #7:**
> **Respond to a speaker without judgment.**

"There are two sides to every story ... at least."

Ann Landers

Use these action steps to accomplish this technique:

- Accept the speaker's communication as worthwhile even though you may not agree.

- Suspend judgment until you have heard all sides of the story.

- Ask questions to get all the facts.

- Mentally check your biases if you find yourself judging what the speaker has to say or arguing with him.

- Do not feel that you have to accept what the speaker says, but do feel that you have to give the speaker a fair chance to explain his point of view.

- Do not fill in the gaps of the communication with your own ideas, thoughts, biases and opinions.

> **Effective Listening Technique #8:**
> **Do not prepare your response**
> **while someone is still talking.**

Try these action steps to accomplish this technique:

- If you know the topic ahead of time, list your arguments before you enter the meeting.

- If you know the biases of the speaker, list those before entering the meeting.

- Wait until after the speaker has finished to formulate your response.

> **Effective Listening Technique #9:**
> **Do not go into a communication situation**
> **with your mind already made up.**

Follow these action steps to accomplish this technique:

- If you know the communication situation ahead of time, list your opinions or preconclusions on a sheet of paper. Then physically tear them up or scratch them out.

- List the situations you expect to come up and your anticipated responses.

"To say the right thing at the right time, keep still most of the time."

John W. Roper

Effective Listening Technique #10:
Negotiate behavior with yourself.
Understand ahead of time what your options
may be to certain words or ideas.
This is not prejudging, this is preparing.

Action Step to Accomplish This Technique

Directions: List a behavior that you anticipate in an upcoming listening situation, such as a meeting. Then indicate what your response will be to that behavior.

Anticipated Behavior	My Response
Cindy's insistence on leading	*Let her have her way to facilitate meeting*

> **Effective Listening Technique #11:**
> **If you realize you are not listening, physically move forward in your seat. If standing, move toward the speaker if possible.**

Use these action steps to accomplish this technique:

- Choose a straight-backed rather than a padded chair if possible.

- Fidget unobtrusively. Move your toes in your shoes instead of tapping your foot, for example.

- Move to another location or shift your position.

Effective Listening Technique #12:
Do not rely on others to interpret what
happened in a meeting or what was said.

Action Step to Accomplish This Technique

Directions: Summarize what happened at a recent meeting. Compare your
summary and conclusion with those of others at the meeting. Are
they the same? If not, why aren't they?

My Conclusions	My Co-Workers' Conclusions

Active Listening takes several different factors into consideration. First, you must learn to listen to the content of the speaker. Second, you must learn to listen to the intent of the speaker. Then you must assess the speaker's nonverbal communication while you monitor your nonverbal communication and filters. Finally, you must learn to listen to the speaker with empathy and without judgment. Each of these factors is equally important and will be explored further in chapters to follow.

Review Questions:

1. What areas on the listening inventory do you need to work on?

2. What are the five steps of Active Listening?

3. What does listening to the content of the speaker mean?

4. What does listening to the intent of the speaker mean?

5. Why is assessing the speaker's nonverbal communication important?

6. Why is monitoring your nonverbal communication and filters important?

7. How do you listen with empathy and without judgment?

8. What have you learned that you can apply today?

Emotional and Mental Filters That Affect Listening

> *"Truth is one forever absolute, but opinion is truth filtered through the moods, the blood, the definitions, of the spectators."*
>
> *Wendall Phillips*

Emotional and mental filters are two factors that affect listening. They are mindsets that were formed, generally, in your childhood. Unless you decide to control them, all that you hear is filtered through them.

Emotional and Mental Filters

Your communication is affected by your emotional and mental filters. They cause you to hear selectively and prevent you from listening actively and objectively. Your immediate mindset filters everything through your current concerns: your expectations, present personal relationships and something as simple as what has happened immediately before the conversation.

Example:

Ned, whose desk is next to yours, says, "My wife and I are thinking about buying a condo. We've had it with all that yard work. It's such a hassle. We figure a condo is the best of both worlds, apartment responsibilities and homeowner equity. What do you think?" How you answer depends on your mindset unless you're actively listening to what Ned says. If you've grown up in a small town where there are few if any apartments, you may have trouble hearing the advantages of condo living. If you've grown up on the farm, you may have trouble hearing someone talk about the hassle of yard work. If you've just come through a messy divorce where owning a home was a headache, you may have trouble understanding why anyone would even want to own a condo. All of these are emotional or mental filters that get in the way of you listening to Ned.

Long-Term Mindset Filters

Your long-term mindset filters everything through your personal background: your values, your past experiences and even your earliest childhood memories. If you've grown up in a culturally diverse neighborhood, you will see and hear things differently than if you have grown up on an isolated ranch in Montana. Your friends and family, your schooling, your religion, your race and your ethnic background are among the many factors that form your long-term mindset filters.

Mini Case Study:

Meg is told by her boss that she has a chance for advancement in the company. It would include a 20 percent pay hike but would require her to locate overseas for two years. The overseas position is in an unstable part of the world, but the company would pay an additional 10 percent because of the location. In preparation Meg would also have to take a six-week intensive language course that would take her away from her family. Her family would be allowed to relocate overseas but housing is hard to find for a family.

Case Study Questions:

1. If Meg values adventure, how will she hear what her boss is saying?

2. If Meg values the family, how will she hear what her boss is saying?

3. If Meg loves money, how will she hear what her boss is saying?

C A S E   S T U D Y

Immediate Emotional and Mental Filters

Definition:

> Immediate filters are those that change depending on current situations. They may be influenced by your long-term filters, but for the most part these are factors that you are immediately concerned with.

Four factors govern your immediate filters.

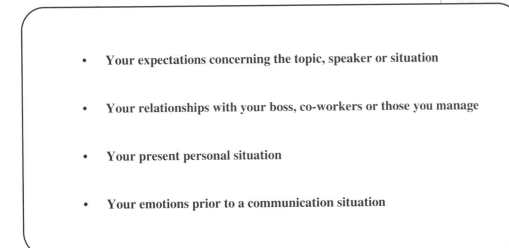

- **Your expectations concerning the topic, speaker or situation**

- **Your relationships with your boss, co-workers or those you manage**

- **Your present personal situation**

- **Your emotions prior to a communication situation**

Your Expectations Concerning the Topic, Speaker or Situation

The expectations you carry into a communication situation can affect your ability to actively listen to what a speaker is saying. For example, you may go into a meeting expecting one thing, but become frustrated because the meeting didn't live up to your expectations.

Example #1:

These expectations may be about the topic. You expect the presenter at a meeting to take a particular stand on a topic or reach a certain conclusion. When he or she starts to talk, you assume you know what's going to be said and listen selectively to support your expectations. You don't listen objectively to what he or she is saying and interpret the information accordingly.

Example #2:

Your expectations also may be about the speaker. Part of these expectations are based on your previous experience with the speaker. "Oh, she's always boring" or "He's overbearing" are examples of expectations you may have.

Example #3:

There are also certain roles that you expect people to fall into because of their status or job description. These expectations can also stifle communication. If your boss doesn't act the way you expect a boss to, your expectations will filter what you hear him or her saying.

Example #4:

Your expectations also may relate to a particular situation. You've probably caught yourself saying, "Oh, no, not another boring meeting," or "I wish I didn't have to go to that party. It will just be a bunch of meaningless small talk." When you catch yourself saying something like this, you are expressing your negative expectations for the situation. If you go into the situation with expectations in full swing, you create a self-fulfilling prophecy. Regardless of the reality of the situation, the meeting will be boring and you will "hear" only the meaningless small talk at the party.

Expectations Worksheet

Directions: Think of the last speaker you heard and answer these
               questions.

1.   What stand did I expect the speaker to take?

2.   What role did I expect the speaker to play because of his or her
      position?

3.   What expectations did I have because of my previous experience
      with the speaker?

4.   What expectations did I have because of the situation?

Use these techniques to control your expectations:

- Before your next meeting or conversation, make a list of what you expect out of the topic, the situation or the speaker. This list represents the barriers that prevent you from actively listening and being able to communicate effectively.

- Test your reactions prior to the meeting or conversation. Anticipate your reactions to particular ideas or situations. Try to predict a full range of responses. Ask yourself, "If he says this, how will I respond?" This is particularly useful in situations where you have had some difficulty in communicating effectively or where you anticipate hearing information that will make you uncomfortable.

Example:

If you tend to approach an annual performance review defensively, determine in advance your strengths and weaknesses and write them down. During the review, stay focused on facts, not emotions.

Reactions Worksheet

Directions: **List what you think the speaker will say in your next meeting. Then write down what your response will be.**

If he or she says *my performance is poor*, **my response is** *Would you go over that with me so I can see how to improve?* .

If he or she says _____,
my response is _____.

If he or she says _____,
my response is _____.

Your Relationships with Your Boss, Co-Workers or Those You Manage

> **Relationships can be made or broken depending on your expectations.**

There are two basic rules when it comes to expectations and relationships.

1. **The more you dislike a person, the harder it is to listen to him objectively.**

2. **The more you like a person, the harder it is to actively listen to him objectively.**

In both cases, the relationship colors the communication. For example, if you intensely dislike your manager, you will have a hard time listening to what he says, even if it makes sense and is in your favor. You will have an equally hard time listening to a person you really like. If he says something you don't agree with, you dismiss it as a mistake. Neither of these situations lends itself to effective communication, particularly in business. Filtering information through positive or negative biases leads to ineffective communication. Set aside your feelings and actively and objectively listen to what is being said.

"I ran against a prejudice that quite cut off the view."

Charlotte Gilman

Relationship Worksheet

Directions: Fill in the blanks below to help you analyze how your relationship with a person affects your ability to listen to that person.

My relationship with _____*Pat*_____ colors my communication with her because _*she's my best friend*_____ . When she talks my reaction is to _*agree with everything she says*_____ .

My relationship with _____ colors my communication with him/her because _____. When he/she talks my reaction is to_____.

My relationship with _____ colors my communication with him/her because _____. When he/she talks my reaction is to_____.

My relationship with _____ colors my communication with him/her because _____. When he/she talks my reaction is to_____.

My relationship with _____ colors my communication with him/her because _____. When he/she talks my reaction is to_____.

Your Current Personal Situation

Our personal situation affects what we hear. If you are experiencing a negative thing such as a job loss or a divorce, you will bring that emotional mindset to your listening situation. If you are experiencing a positive thing such as a promotion or an engagement, you will bring that mindset to your listening. If your personal life is happy, you will tend to view the rest of the world in a more positive light.

Key Idea:

> You cannot separate your personal situation from your career, but you can control how it filters information by keeping your professional and personal lives as separate as possible.

Follow These Techniques to Help Separate Your Personal and Professional Lives

- When you are at work, distance yourself mentally or physically from your personal life. If you can, leave the office gossip at work. Deal with only personal emergencies during the work day. Throw yourself into your work at your workplace to help distance yourself from your personal life. Visualize your work life in a box with your personal life surrounding it but not in it.

- If you commute, use that time to leave your personal life at home.

- Practice self-talk. Telling yourself that you are a good employee, even though your personal life may be crumbling around you, can keep you on track at work.

    Self-Talk Scripts:

    - "I am a good employee."
    - "I am good at my job."
    - "I enjoy my work."
    - "I can do anything I set my mind to."
    - "Today will be a good day."
    - "I work well with others."

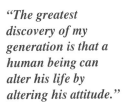

> *"The greatest discovery of my generation is that a human being can alter his life by altering his attitude."*
>
> *William James*

45

> *"This makes me so sore it gits my dandruff up."*
>
> *Samuel Goldwyn*

- Share your personal concerns with someone who can help you clarify them.

How Your Immediate Emotional Mindset Affects a Communication Situation

Often in a situation where you ought to be actively listening, you are angry or upset about something that has happened immediately before. This emotional baggage gets in the way of Active Listening.

Example:

Answering the telephone when you are in the middle of a heated discussion will hamper your ability to listen effectively during the first few moments on the phone. Your mind still will be dealing with the heated discussion.

Key Idea:

To switch gears quickly, you need to detach yourself emotionally from the previous situation.

Here Are Some Techniques to Detach Yourself Emotionally from the Previous Situation:

- Create a buffer zone if possible. This involves spending a few minutes engaged in a neutral activity such as filing or sorting your mail. These activities allow you to detach yourself from your negative emotions before you have to interact with others.

- If time and circumstances permit, exercise. Take a brisk, five-minute walk.

- Take a coffee break and let your mind wander for five minutes.

- Count to 10 and breathe deeply.

- Let the phone go four or five rings so that you have time to switch gears.

Summary

You can control your immediate emotional and mental filters by:

- Knowing your expectations of the speaker

- Recognizing how your relationship with the speaker affects your response

- Assessing your personal situation and how it affects what you hear

- Detaching yourself emotionally from the previous situations

Long-Term Filters

The immediate filters that affect Active Listening are probably the ones you are most aware of. It's easy to know what made you angry 10 minutes ago. The long-term filters, however, are so much a part of who you are that you may not even realize they are operating.

Definition:

> Long-term filters are formed by your values, religious upbringing, culture, the region you grew up in and even your parents' political biases. They are the filters that you learned as a child.

Example:

> You were brought up in a conservative Jewish home in Chicago. Your family home was in a middle-class, predominantly Jewish suburb and your parents were both active in the Republican party. You take a job in Milwaukee. During the first week your boss keeps referring to his children going to CCD class. He asks you if you would be willing to be on the committee to plan the annual Christmas party. You have trouble hearing him because you don't know anything about CCD classes until you ask and find that they are the Catholic equivalent of Hebrew School. You are incensed by him asking you to help plan the Christmas party.

> *"Speak when you're angry — and you'll make the best speech you'll ever regret."*
>
> *Laurence J. Peter*

If you find yourself reacting emotionally to something that is being communicated and you know it's not because of your expectations, a personal relationship with the speaker, your personal situation or a reaction to something immediately before, then your long-term filters are probably the culprit.

Identifying Your Long-Term Filters

Directions: Think of a recent communication situation that affected you emotionally and answer the following questions.

1.   Did the speaker remind you of someone from your past in action, tone of voice or word choice? Did that recollection trigger an emotional response?

2.   Did the situation remind you of a similar incident in the past?

3.   Was your reaction the result of a conflict of personal, religious, political or philosophical values? What was that conflict?

4.   Was your emotional reaction driven by a specific prejudice or bias?

Example of How Long-Term Filters Affect Your Listening

Your best friend at work says, "I've decided not to try for the promotion to shop foreman. I don't want all the troubles that go along with it. I'll just stay here on the line where I can do an honest day's work and have none of the headaches of management." How you react to him depends on your long-term emotional filters. If you were brought up with a strong work ethic, you will hear, "...where I can do an honest day's work..." If you were taught that a person should always better himself, you will have trouble hearing your friend's reasoning for not wanting to advance. If you are going to actively listen, you must suspend judgment, and if you are truly upset with what he says, the last thing you want is to close down communication. If he sees that you are listening to what he is saying, he in turn is more likely to listen to you.

Key Idea:

> With long-term filters, the more you understand yourself—your values, your past experiences and even your earliest childhood memories—the better you will be able to listen with empathy and without judging those with whom you disagree. Naturally, if these long-term filters seriously impede your ability to function, you should seek professional help. However, a basic understanding of them will help in your quest to become a better listener.

Summary

> Emotional and mental filters do not leave us. They are a natural part of the way we function. To become a better listener you need to learn how to identify and control the filters that get in the way of actively listening.

"He flattered himself on being a man without any prejudices; this pretention itself is a very great prejudice."

Anatole France

These Are the Key Areas That Influence Your Emotional and Mental Filters:

- Your expectations

- Your personal relationships

- Your past experiences

- Your values and biases

Practice These Keys to Control Your Filters:

- Identify them.

- Separate yourself from them mentally or physically to minimize their influence.

- Concentrate on keeping an open mind as you listen.

Summary

One of the keys to becoming an Active Listener is learning to identify and control your immediate and long-term filters. Without controlling them you will only be able to selectively listen, thus impeding your ability to effectively listen to those around you.

Review Questions:

1. What immediate emotional and mental filters do I have?

2. What techniques can be used to control immediate emotional and mental filters?

3. What long-term filters do I have?

4. What techniques can be used to control my long-term filters?

CHAPTER 4

Common Barriers to Listening and How to Overcome Them

Other factors that can impair your ability to listen effectively are internal and external barriers. Barriers are not filters. Your brain filters what information to use. Barriers stop the information or interfere with it before it reaches the brain.

Definition:

Barriers are things that get in the way of your ability to listen.

With emotional and mental filters, you listen selectively. In most cases, barriers can be controlled so that you may practice Active Listening.

> ### There Are Two Types of Barriers:
>
> - **External**
> - **Mental**

External Barriers

> **Three Types of External Barriers:**
>
> - **Physical Objects**
> - **Noise**
> - **Movement**

Key Idea:

External barriers can be controlled, particularly if you have control over your work environment.

Physical Barriers

Definition:

Physical barriers distance you by blocking your view of the speaker or by distracting you from watching and listening to the speaker.

Example #1:

You will find it harder to actively listen in a large meeting, such as a stockholders' meeting, if you sit in the back of the room. Even a public address system won't help, because you will have a hard time "reading" the speaker's body language from a distance.

Example #2:

In a one-on-one meeting, a desk between you and the other person acts as a physical barrier. It immediately sends the message that the person behind the desk is guarded in his communication. The desk also makes reading nonverbal communication more difficult.

Example #3:

Lack of eye contact is another external barrier to effective communication because it diminishes a sense of trust between speaker and listener. If you cannot see the eyes of the speaker, perhaps because he or she is wearing dark glasses or refuses to make eye contact, you will not have the full benefit of Active Listening.

Example #4:

Communicating through writing and by telephone are physical barriers to Active Listening. You have eliminated the opportunity to observe body language and, in the case of correspondence, hear the other person's tone of voice.

Directions: **List physical barriers to listening you encounter at work. Writing them down will make you more aware of them.**

Physical Barriers to Listening in My Workplace

Desk

Telephone

Use These Techniques to Eliminate Physical Barriers:

- Sit or stand where you can maintain eye contact with a speaker.

- Sit or stand where you can read the body language of all the members of a group.

- Don't send the message that you have "tuned out" by moving your chair backwards, leaning back in your chair or by stacking material between you and the speaker.

- If you take notes, keep them to a minimum by focusing on the key points. After the meeting or conversation, summarize what happened.

- If you receive a handout, refer to it mainly when the speaker refers to it. If possible, set it in a place where its physical presence will not distract you from listening. If it is essential that you understand the handout, ask the speaker to give you time to read it. This will allow you to concentrate on only one thing at a time.

- If you are wearing dark glasses, remove them to optimize eye contact with the speaker.

- When conducting one-on-one conversations in an office, try to avoid sitting behind a desk or across a table.

Try to overcome these listening barriers one at a time. Don't overwhelm yourself by trying to eliminate all of them at once.

"Speech was made to open man to man, and not to hide him."

David Lloyd

Noise and Movement

Two common barriers to Active Listening that affect us daily are noise and movement. The ability to block out noise varies among individuals, but even the best listener has trouble blocking it out occasionally. In the general population 80 percent will automatically block out background noise and movement. Some people block out background noise outside their immediate area but are distracted by noise near them. Others can listen if the noise is constant, like the whir of a ceiling fan. Still others are highly distracted by virtually all noise. Some are distracted by only high- or low-pitched noises. For some, noise is not a problem. They, instead, are distracted by movement. Both are serious barriers to Active Listening.

> **The louder the noise, the bolder the movement, the more distracting it is.**

Key Idea:

If you find yourself listening to other conversations while you are trying to concentrate, you may be among the people who are distracted by noise. If you get less done in a visually active room than in a private office, you are probably distracted by movement.

Noise/Movement Inventory

Directions: Indicate after each statement how often it is true for you. By identifying the types of distractions that affect you, you will better understand and control them and become a more effective listener.

Noise/Movement	Never	Rarely	Sometimes	Often	Always
I am distracted by loud noises.					
I am distracted by high-pitched noises.					
I am distracted by low-pitched noises.					
I am distracted by noises near me, but not those outside my immediate work area.					
I am distracted by all noises except constant ones like those made by fans.					
I am distracted by human voices.					
I am distracted by non-human sounds.					
I am distracted by movement near me.					
I am distracted by movement within my peripheral vision.					
I am distracted by random movement, but not constant movement.					

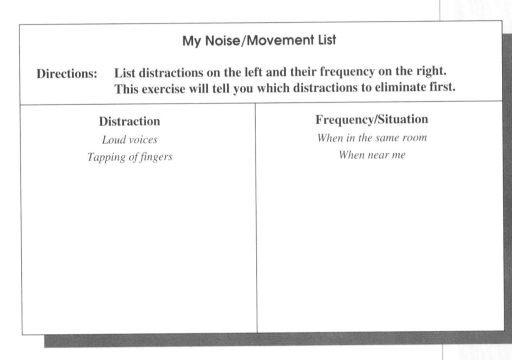

My Noise/Movement List

Directions: List distractions on the left and their frequency on the right. This exercise will tell you which distractions to eliminate first.

Distraction	**Frequency/Situation**
Loud voices	*When in the same room*
Tapping of fingers	*When near me*

Try These Techniques to Control Noise and Movement Barriers to Listening:

If possible, eliminate noise from your work environment by following these suggestions.

- Turn off or turn down radios or canned music.

- Turn down the ringer on your phone or intercom.

- Shut your office door when having a conversation.

- Tell your secretary to limit interruptions when you need to concentrate on listening.

- Place yourself close to the speaker in a meeting and away from noise distractions, such as fellow workers talking, office sounds and the hum of air conditioning units.

- Turn your head away from the noise if you're trying to concentrate on a telephone conversation.

- Ask those making the noise to be more quiet. Be polite when making your request.

"Silence is golden."

Thomas Carlyle

If possible, eliminate movement in your workplace by trying some of these suggestions.

- Place yourself in a cubicle or with your back to the movement.

- Close your eyes to block out the movement if you're talking on the phone.

- During a meeting or lecture, sit where your ability to see movement is minimized.

- Ask those making the movement to stop. Be polite when making the request.

- Rearrange your office so that movement distraction is at a minimum.

- Install blinds or curtains on windows to block outside movement.

- Close your office door so you can concentrate on the speaker.

Case Study:

Bob is interrupted on a regular basis when speaking with and listening to his co-workers. His office is small. His desk faces a door that is usually open and an inside window with blinds that are usually open, too. He has piped-in music with speaker controls, a phone/intercom, a computer, filing cabinets and bookcases. Behind his desk there is a floor-to-ceiling window with drapes that usually are open. The window looks out on the street 15 stories below. Immediately outside his office is an area where several clerks/typists sit, including his own secretary, who has an extremely loud voice and a tendency to talk nonstop. Beyond this area, in full view from Bob's office, is a main corridor and two elevators.

C A S E   S T U D Y

Case Study Questions:

1. Which of the physical barriers to Active Listening does Bob have control of?

2. What action can he take to eliminate those physical barriers?

3. Which of the noise/movement barriers to Active Listening does Bob have control of?

4. What action can he take to eliminate those noise/movement barriers?

Mental Barriers

Mental barriers, like emotional filters, are internal. However, unlike emotional filters, mental distractions do not selectively sort or alter the information you receive. They simply block your ability to receive any information. The amount of your control over mental distractions will depend on the amount of control you have over your mind and emotions.

Here Are Some Common Mental Distractions:

- **Fear** — For example, if you fear that you are going to lose your job, you are less likely to listen carefully.

- **Worry** — Worrying about things such as family matters or whether you're going to meet performance standards at work can impede listening.

- **Being unprepared** — You are less likely to listen carefully because you are worried about being unprepared.

- **Daydreaming** — It's easy to find your mind wandering.

- **Boredom** — When you are bored you are more likely to daydream.

- **Poor self-esteem** — Poor self-esteem may affect listening because you are worried about what others think of you. Emotional and mental filters tend to block out the positives that you hear about yourself.

- **Anger** — Anger is an overpowering emotion that clouds your ability to listen carefully. Additionally, your emotional and mental filters can be affected by anger.

Mental Distractions

Directions: For each mental distraction listed below, indicate how frequently it affects you.

Mental Distraction	Never	Rarely	Sometimes	Often	Always
Fear					
Worry					
Being unprepared					
Daydreaming					
Boredom					
Poor self-esteem					
Anger					

Mental distractions may change depending on your personal situation. For example, you may daydream because you have already heard a presentation or you may not be able to concentrate because you are worried about a presentation you have to make later in the day. In both cases, you are using Inactive Listening. Mental distractions have blocked your ability to hear what the speaker is saying.

Use These Techniques to Control Mental Barriers:

- Identify the distraction.

- Write down what is distracting you and promise yourself you will deal with it later.

- Organize for meetings. The more prepared you are, the more you can actively listen.

- Take notes if you find yourself daydreaming.

- Relate what is being said to your own situation if you become bored. Also try taking notes. They force you to listen and sort out the essential and nonessential information.

- Write down what is making you angry and deal with it later.

- If worrying about something is keeping you from actively listening, write down the worst outcome you can think of. This should show you how ridiculous the worry really is.

- Come to each meeting fresh. Try to get enough sleep, exercise and healthful food so that you are mentally alert.

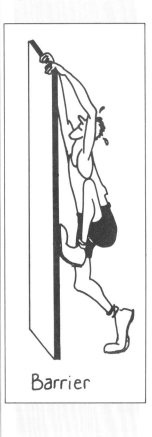

Barrier

C A S E   S T U D Y

Case Study:

Ellen is in charge of 12 salespeople in her division. Lately, she has had trouble listening to them as they present their sales figures at the weekly divisional meeting. She finds herself thinking how uninteresting the figures are. Sometimes she imagines herself on a plane for Tahiti. On other days, she worries whether her performance as a manager is as good as it could be. Unfortunately, these thoughts erode her self-esteem and she becomes angry with herself for thinking this way. Meanwhile, the salespeople continue their reports while Ellen picks up only bits and pieces. Luckily, the reports are also written, so she can review them later. However, she sometimes finds herself asking a salesperson to repeat what was just said.

Case Study Questions:

1. What mental distractions is Ellen experiencing?
2. Which ones can she control?
3. What techniques can she use to eliminate those distractions?

Summary

In most cases, external and internal distractions can be controlled. To become an Active Listener you will need to identify those distractions that block your listening and try to control them. Fortunately, distractions are easier to identify and control than emotional filters because they are usually much less permanent.

Review Questions:

1. What is a physical distraction?

2. What is a mental distraction?

3. Which physical and mental distractions affect my ability to listen?

4. Which physical and mental distractions can I control?

5. What is my action plan for controlling physical and mental distractions?

CHAPTER 5

Reflective Listening

Now and again you need a person to talk to, someone to help you talk out a problem, someone who is a good listener. You don't want this person to argue with you or discuss or even give advice. You just want someone to listen to what you are saying. The person you need is a reflective listener.

Definition:

> Reflective Listening keys on the speaker's content, intent and nonverbals and does so with empathy and without judgment.

Purpose of Reflective Listening

Reflective Listening mirrors what the speaker is saying by reflecting back to the speaker, thus allowing him to gain a fresh perspective on what he has communicated, both verbally and nonverbally. This helps him better understand what he is trying to communicate. For example, when the speaker says, "I'm so angry with my secretary, I'd like to fire her," the reflective listener says, "I hear you saying your secretary's made you angry." He reflects back what the speaker is saying. His reflection helps the speaker hear what others hear him saying.

Reflective Listening is usually used in one-on-one situations when the speaker is trying to solve a problem or think through an idea. Occasionally, you will use Reflective Listening in a group situation to help clarify what the speaker is saying.

> *"The right word may be effective, but no word was ever as effective as a rightly-timed pause."*
>
> *Mark Twain*

Key Idea:

Reflective Listening should not be overused. However, it is extremely valuable in helping you understand the ideas, problems and frustrations of others. By listening reflectively, you allow people to solve their own problems rather than letting their problems become yours. When someone comes to you with a problem, ask yourself, "Whose problem is it?" If it's yours, solve it. If it is the other person's, listen reflectively so he or she can solve it.

Here Are Three Key Steps to Reflective Listening:

1. Practice good Active Listening skills so you understand what the speaker is trying to communicate.

2. Provide feedback to the speaker. Rephrase what the speaker just said so that he knows what he's just said.

3. Make sure the feedback is expressed with empathy and without judgment. By rephrasing what the speaker said, you avoid judging him. If you are empathic, you validate the speaker. If you are nonjudgmental, you help him decide whether what he says is wise. If he wants your advice, he'll ask for it.

Case Study:

Sam is considered a good listener and consequently his peers seek him out. One Monday morning the following conversation took place between Sam and Martin on the way to work.

Martin: "You know, Sam, I've about had it with Larry. He keeps stealing my accounts, and it's burning me up."

Sam: "I hear what you're saying."

Martin: "Just last Friday I found out that he'd done it again. He said something about the fact that it was his account originally."

Sam: "When I hear you say that Larry's stealing your accounts, I wonder why you say that."

Martin: "Oh, because I've had five accounts that have ended up being his."

Sam: "You must feel slighted by these stolen accounts."

Martin: "Exactly right. How could the company do that to me?"

Sam: "I hear you saying that the company is hurting you. Is there a possibility that the company is reassigning these so that you'll have more time to devote to your major accounts?"

Martin: "I never thought of that."

Case Study Questions:

1. How did Sam phrase his questions so that Martin felt he was being listened to?

2. How did Sam phrase his last question so that Martin saw another point of view?

3. Did Sam ever place blame on anyone, including Martin or the company?

4. Did Sam intensify Martin's anger with his questions?

5. How did Sam phrase his questions so that Martin did not feel he was being judged?

How to Listen with Empathy

Listening with empathy sends the message that you care about the speaker. However, it does not mean that you agree with the speaker.

Key Idea:

> When you listen with empathy, let the speaker know that you understand his situation or problem. Indicate that you can put yourself in his shoes and feel the way he does. This proves powerful when listening to a frustrated employee or teenager, because it puts you in a nonadversarial position.

Verbal and Nonverbal Techniques for Listening with Empathy

The following are just a few sample responses that you may find useful when listening to a friend or business associate with a problem.

Verbal Responses:

- "I understand what you're saying."

- "I see your point."

- "I've been there myself."

- "I know where you're coming from."

- "I know you really mean that."

Action Worksheet

Directions: Listed below are statements someone made to you. Write a response that is empathic to the speaker.

"Teresa is really getting on my nerves. She never returns my calls."

Sample Response: *"I understand what you're saying."*

"My boss thinks that I'm aggressive."

Response:

"If I have to go to another production meeting, I think I'll scream!"

Response:

"I just don't understand why I'm always chosen to work overtime, while Mike never has to."

Response:

Nonverbal responses are used in almost any situation. They are effective when a friend or business associate needs someone to listen to him, but he doesn't need much of a verbal response. These responses show that you are listening and that you care.

Nonverbal Responses:

- Nod your head to indicate that you really understand what the speaker is saying.
- Touch the speaker to comfort him if it's appropriate to the situation.
- Lean or step forward to show that you are interested.
- Maintain eye contact.

My Empathic Listening Inventory

Directions: **Place a check mark beside each response that is appropriate.**

Within the last week I have used the following empathic phrases:

- ❏ "I understand what you're saying."
- ❏ "I see your point."
- ❏ "I've been there myself."
- ❏ "I know where you're coming from."
- ❏ "I know you really mean that."

Within the last week I have used the following empathic nonverbal signals:

- ❏ I nodded my head to show that I really understood what the speaker was saying.
- ❏ I touched the speaker to comfort him in an appropriate situation.
- ❏ I leaned or stepped forward to show that I was interested.
- ❏ I maintained eye contact.

Summary:

By using these techniques, you are creating a comfort zone for the speaker. The message you are sending is that you care about what he or she has to say.

How to Listen Without Judging

Listening without judging is perhaps the hardest thing to do when practicing both Active and Reflective Listening. We naturally judge the communication we hear based on our emotional and mental filters.

Key Idea:

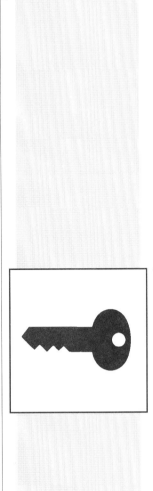

> To listen without judging, you have to learn to set aside preconceived ideas and opinions.
>
> Listening in a nonjudgmental way will help everyone involved communicate better. Do not go into a listening situation prepared for a battle that you've got to win. Go into a listening situation prepared for a win-win outcome for you and the speaker. Listening without judging will help you accomplish that.
>
> How you respond to the speaker is the true measure of your ability to listen without passing judgment.

Use These Techniques to Respond Without Judgment:

- **The Simple "I" Message:**

    The simple "I" message rephrases the speaker's message into your own words. It is descriptive.

    Example #1:

    A co-worker comes to you and says that he is upset with the way his supervisor is treating him. It seems like his supervisor is giving him more work than everyone else. Your "I" message would be something

> *"Keep strong, if possible. In any case, keep cool. Have unlimited patience ... Put yourself in his shoes — so as to see things through his eyes."*
>
> **Basil H. L. Hart**

like, "I hear you saying John is giving you more work than everyone else."

Example #2:

Your co-worker says, "I hate this job. There's never enough time for my family. All I do is go to work, stay late every evening to do paperwork and come home exhausted." Your "I" message might say, "I get the impression you're feeling a lot of pressure from your job."

Simple "I" messages restate what you think the speaker is saying or feeling.

Once you have responded with a simple "I" message, then it's the speaker's turn to respond. In these examples you have responded in a nonjudgmental way, even though you may personally think that the first co-worker's complaint is unfounded and that the second co-worker could learn to manage his workday better.

- **The Feeling Message:**

Sometimes an "I" message is not enough. In a supercharged situation filled with emotion, you may want to try a feeling message.

Example #3:

A co-worker is angry about her boss and says, "I don't know how Mr. Clark can hate me so. He showed Meredith the list of people attending the convention in L.A. and she said I'm not on it. I just know he's against me."

Questions:

1. Whose problem is this?

2. How would you respond?

Analysis:

The problem is your co-worker's, but as a close friend you may want to make it your problem, too. If you listen reflectively, you will help her understand and deal with the problem herself. In this case you may want to use a feeling message as part of your Reflective Listening.

Try These Techniques for a Feeling Message:

Give yourself time to think. Ask yourself, "What is my co-worker feeling?" and "Why is she feeling this way?"

Formula for a feeling message:

> **"You feel** _____
>
> **because** _____**."**

Fill in the blanks by reflecting back the feelings and the reasons for the feelings as you understand them.

Feeling Message for Example #1:

- "You feel your supervisor is against you because he appears to be giving you more work than the others."

Feeling Messages for Example #2:

- "You feel that you hate this job because you never have time for your family."

- "You feel that you're missing out on your family because of this job."

Feeling Messages for Example #3:

- "You feel hurt because your name was not on the convention list."

- "You feel Mr. Clark hates you because your name wasn't on the list."

> *"Silence gives consent, or a horrible feeling that nobody's listening."*
>
> *Franklin P. Jones*

Key Idea:

Feeling messages help clarify emotional statements. The key to feeling messages is that you don't become emotional yourself. Keep your feelings in check. If you're emotional, then you're not listening reflectively.

Feeling Message Worksheet

Directions: Respond with a feeling message to the following situations.

"If there's anything I hate, it's an employee who's always late. Once again, you're late."

> **Sample Response:** *"I hear you saying that you're unhappy with me because I'm late."*

"My secretary can't get anything right. I'm losing important messages!"

> **Response:**

"Dad, you don't even care enough about me to come to my game. All you care about is work."

> **Response:**

"Just who do you think you are, brown-nosing the boss like that?"

> **Response:**

- **Active "I" Message:**

    Definition:

    The active "I" message is an "I" message that moves
    from Reflective Listening to Active Listening.

    Key Idea:

    The active "I" message is used when you want the
    speaker to know how you feel about what he is talking
    about, rather than simply reflecting back what he says.

Example #3 Recap:

Your co-worker is angry and says, "I don't know how Mr.
Clark can hate me so. He showed Meredith the list of people
going to the convention in L.A. and she said I'm not on it. I
just know he's against me."

Using this example, an active "I" message would be, "When
you talk about how Mr. Clark hates you, I'm concerned
because I think you're basing your decision on incomplete
information."

Example # 4:

Your office manager comes to you complaining about how
slow your secretary is in getting work back to him. He is
obviously angry and your secretary's performance is affecting
you. An active "I" message to your boss might be, "When you
come to me upset about my secretary's performance, I feel like
it's my fault. Is that what you are trying to say?"

Example # 5:

You are having lunch at the construction site of a new office
building you are working on. Your co-worker Mick says,
"Why are you always shoving all your crap off on me. I've got
enough to do without doing your job, too." You are surprised
that Mick has confronted you. You've been covering for him
because he's not been feeling well. Your active "I" message to
him is, "When you tell me you're doing my job, I get confused.
I've been trying to cover for you while you've been sick."

Key Idea:

The active "I" message tells the speaker that you hear what he or she is saying and this is how you feel about it. You are not judging the person. You are simply saying what you think.

Active "I" Message Worksheet

Directions: Respond to the following statements using an active "I" message.

"If there's anything I hate, it's an employee who's always late. Once again, you're late."

Sample Response: *"When you say I'm always late, I get frustrated. I've been late just three times in the last three months. Isn't that acceptable according to company policy?"*

"My secretary can't get anything right. I'm losing important messages!"
Response:

"Dad, you don't even care enough about me to come to my game. All you care about is work."
Response:

"Just who do you think you are, brown-nosing the boss like that?"
Response:

Open-Ended Questions

Definition:

An open-ended question is one that does not have a right or
wrong answer, nor can it be answered with one or two words.
An open-ended question forces the speaker to rethink what he
is saying. When you are listening reflectively, you may need to
ask open-ended questions to further understand the speaker's
message.

Rewriting Closed-Ended Questions into Open-Ended Questions

Directions: Rewrite each of the following closed-ended questions so it becomes
open-ended. A closed-ended question can be answered simply, quite
often with a one-word answer such as "Yes" or "No."

1. **Do you think they will eliminate our department?**

    Sample Rewrite: *What do you think about the possibility of eliminating
    our department?*

    Your Rewrite:

2. **Are you concerned about finding a job?**

    Rewrite:

3. **Who was in charge of this account?**

    Rewrite:

4. **Does your boss know you are angry with him?**

    Rewrite:

5. **When should you have this done?**

    Rewrite:

Three Guiding Principles for Responding Without Judgment

1. Respond to the behavior or idea, not the speaker.

2. Respond in the present, not the past.

3. Respond by describing, not evaluating.

**Respond to the behavior or idea,
not the speaker.**

By responding to the speaker's behavior or the ideas, you avoid responding to the personality of the speaker. It is the same principle used to respond to a 7-year-old when he's done something wrong. For example, "I like you, but I don't like it when you ride your bike in the street."

Key Idea:

Ideas and behavior are neutral and negotiable topics. Personalities are not. More than likely you are not going to be able to change someone's personality. People can, however, change their ideas and behavior.

Response Worksheet

Directions: Give an empathic and/or nonjudgmental response to each of the following situations.

1. Zoe is angry because her husband accused her of wrecking the car when she had a fender bender. She arrives at the office, slamming file cabinet drawers left and right.

    Sample Response: *"When you come into the office and slam the file cabinet drawers, I don't understand. Can you tell me who you are angry with?"*

    Your Response:

2. Your boss is holding a meeting. During the reports, she taps her fingers incessantly. She constantly looks around as if she wants to escape. After the meeting is over, she stops you in the hall and says, "These meetings are getting to be a waste of time."

    Response:

3. You arrive home after a long day at the office. You are greeted by an unhappy spouse who thrusts your 2-year-old into your arms and says, "Here, you take him. He just broke the crystal pitcher your mother gave us for our wedding. Do you think you could help out for a change? You're not the only one who brings money home to this family!"

    Response:

> *"The real art of conversation is not only to say the right thing in the right place, but to leave unsaid the wrong thing at the tempting moment."*
>
> *Dorothy Nevill*

Respond in the present, not the past.

Neither you nor the speaker can change the past. You can only deal with the present and try to control the future. Arguing about the past will only cause hard feelings and impede communication.

Example:

If you slip from using Active or Reflective Listening and say something like "You've always been late" or "You're always saying we should close down Quality Control," then you are no longer listening in a nonjudgmental way. Appropriate nonjudgmental responses would be "When you're late, I feel that the others are cheated because we have to wait for you" or "When you suggest that we close down Quality Control, I wonder if you have considered the problems involved in doing that." It doesn't matter how many times the person has been late or has said Quality Control should be closed down. The past can't be changed.

Key Idea:

Deal with the present and avoid absolute statements. No one "always" behaves in a particular way.

Response Rewrite

Directions: Rewrite the following statements so that they respond to the present instead of the past.

1. "It's the same old thing. Nothing's done on time."
    Sample Response: *"Your project is not on time this week."*
    Your Response:

2. "You always say that you're going to fire her, but you don't."
    Response:

3. "Nothing has changed since we met. You still won't budge."
    Response:

4. "You're always griping about your department."
    Response:

5. "For the past two months you've messed up. Last year it was the same thing in January and February."
    Response:

Respond by describing, not evaluating.

Describe what you hear, don't judge what is being said. For example, don't say, "You're just blowing this whole thing out of proportion." While that may be the way you feel, your response immediately puts your co-worker on the defensive. Describing rather than judging the speaker's comment will keep communication lines open. Your response could be, "I hear you say that your name was not on the list that Meredith saw." After making this statement, you can use an open-ended question such as, "How can you find out if your name was or was not on the list?"

Response Rewrite

Directions: Rewrite the following responses so that you describe rather than evaluate.

Ex: "You've got to be kidding. They promoted Smitty?"

Sample Response: *"Did I hear you say that they promoted Smitty?"*

1. "I don't like hearing that you can't trust Mary anymore."
   Response:

2. "In my opinion, Josh is wrong. He really must have wanted to upset Mark."
   Response:

3. "You're sure acting silly about this whole Martinson deal."
   Response:

4. "That's a bunch of bull. Maxine never said she was trying to take over Bev's job."
   Response:

Case Study:

Lucy, who is the lead engineer, comes to you and says, "We've got some real problems with Bert. I think he's drinking, and it affects his work. The other day he was late, and he came in smelling of booze, sort of wobbling down the assembly line. He's been fouling up, and now I have to retool everything. I'll have to come in this weekend if I'm going to make the deadline."

Case Study Questions:

1. Whose problem is this?

2. How would you respond in an empathic way to Lucy?

3. How would you respond in a nonjudgmental way to Lucy?

4. How would you respond with feeling to Lucy?

5. How would you respond to Lucy using an active "I" message?

Summary

Reflective Listening can be a powerful tool when used correctly. If used too often, Reflective Listening will make people feel that everything is a one-way communication and that they are doing all the talking. If used appropriately, Reflective Listening can help you better understand your business associates and family.

When Practicing Reflective Listening, Follow These Tips:

- Respond in a nonjudgmental way.

- Don't force the speaker to share his or her feelings. The speaker may misinterpret your concern and cut off communication.

- Don't overuse Reflective Listening. Save it for the really big issues.

- Take time to listen. It will pay off.

C A S E   S T U D Y

- Try not to ask too many questions. Don't be too nosy or pushy.

- Respond as accurately as you can. Don't lie to make the speaker feel better.

- Respond as honestly as you can.

- Reflect back positive and pleasant feelings. It makes the speaker feel better about himself or herself.

- Don't be disappointed if you aren't a perfect reflective listener.

- Urge the speaker to take the problem to an expert if it's something bigger than both of you can handle.

Review Questions:

1. What are the three steps to Reflective Listening?

2. What is an example of a nonverbal empathic response?

3. What is an example of a simple "I" message?

4. What is an example of an active "I" message?

5. Why are open-ended questions preferable to closed-ended questions?

6. What are the three guiding principles for responding without judgment?

CHAPTER 6

Using Nonverbals to Enhance Communication

Ninety percent of what you communicate is expressed through nonverbal communication. Ninety percent! Fifty-five percent is through body language and 35 percent by the tone of your voice. We tend to think, however, that when we listen, we need listen only to the words of the speaker. The words by themselves are only 10 percent of what the speaker is communicating. When you use Active Listening you assess the speaker's nonverbals and monitor your own. Doing so tells the speaker that you are listening carefully to what he or she is saying.

Key Idea:

> If the speaker thinks you are listening carefully, then communication lines will be kept open.

By listening for his nonverbal communication, you send a signal that says, "I understand you." Even if he doesn't actively listen, he is more likely to respond to you. His body will put him in an Active Listening mode, increasing the chances of understanding what you say.

Of that 90 percent, 55 percent is through body language such as gestures and facial expression. The other 35 percent is by the tone of your voice. In this chapter we will explore how you can use both nonverbal and verbal communication to encourage your speaker.

Using Body Language to Show That You Are Listening

There are a variety of ways you can demonstrate that you are actively listening. For example, you can sit up in your chair and lean forward. This signals that you are listening carefully. Your chin cupped in your hand can tell the speaker that you are thoughtfully considering what is being said. Nodding your head in agreement is also an important gesture that you, the active listener, can use.

Here are some kinds of body language that tell the speaker you are actively listening:

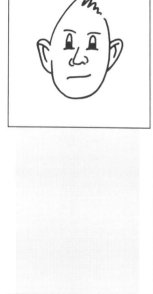

- Facial expressions
- Gestures
- Posture
- Eye contact
- Vocal cues
- Appearance
- Personal space

• Facial Expressions

All of us have learned to mask our true feelings and put on the face that someone else wants to see. Facial expressions, though important in communicating, are also one of the easiest to fake. Since facial expressions can be artificial, you must take special precautions in using and interpreting them.

Examples of Facial Expressions:

You may have encountered the happy face of a food server taking an order even though he has just had angry words with his manager. You may have used the "so-glad-to-see-you-again" face to your boss's boss whom you can't stand. Or you may have seen the face of an employee intent on what an instructor in a seminar is saying while in fact he is daydreaming.

Key Idea:

> Facial expressions can either enhance or impair listening, as well as send conflicting signals.

Research has shown that different cultures convey different meanings through facial expressions. However, the following expressions can be recognized in almost all cultures.

- Happiness
- Anger
- Sadness
- Disgust
- Surprise
- Fear

Facial Expression Exercise

Directions: **Describe the facial expression for each of the following emotions.**

Happiness   *Smile on face*

Anger

Sadness

Disgust

Surprise

Fear

Practice These Tips for Using Facial Expressions:

- Make your facial expression consistent with other nonverbal clues you are giving. For example, if you smile but sit with your fist clenched, you are sending conflicting signals.

- Be aware of the timing of your facial expression. Is it contrived instead of spontaneous?

- Be sure your facial expression supports or reinforces your verbal message. Is it appropriate? If your verbal message is negative, for example, don't smile.

- If you disagree with the speaker, you have two choices. Your facial expression can reflect your disagreement or you may choose to look neutral. Both are valid. Showing disagreement is acceptable as long as it doesn't provoke conflict. A neutral face shows that you are being nonjudgmental.

- Smile if you agree with the speaker.

- Put an "I-don't-understand-what-you're-saying" look on your face if you are confused by what the speaker is saying.

- Use eye contact. A speaker should have eye contact with the audience 60 percent of the time. You, as a listener, can have less eye contact. However, minimal or no eye contact sends the message that you aren't listening.

Facial Expression Checklist

Directions: Analyze a recent listening situation and answer the following questions.

1.   **If I showed disagreement in my facial expression, did it provoke conflict?**   Yes   No

2.   **Did I use a neutral expression even though I disagreed?**   Yes   No

3.   **Did I smile when I agreed?**   Yes   No

4.   **Did I use an "I-don't-understand-what-you're-saying" expression when I was confused by the speaker?**   Yes   No

5.   **Did I maintain eye contact with the speaker?**   Yes   No

• Gestures

Like facial expressions, gestures show that you are listening. Gestures include your posture and upper body movements. If you "talk with your hands," gestures may come naturally. If you don't, you may want to practice using gestures to communicate with a speaker.

Here are some common gestures:

- Pointing your finger
- Throwing your hands up in disgust
- Scratching your head when you don't understand
- Raising your shoulders when you don't understand
- Moving toward the speaker to "listen" better
- Nodding or shaking your head "yes" or "no"
- Tapping your fingers to show boredom or impatience

Gestures Exercise # 1

Directions: Keep track of the gestures made during a business meeting. Indicate what they seem to communicate. Concentrate on only the gestures — leave the other nonverbal signals for another time. When the meeting is over, examine your interpretations.

Gesture	What It Communicates
Slightly tilted head with quizzical expression on face	*Curiosity*

Another gesture that can affect the way you listen is someone's handshake. A handshake helps form an impression that can then affect your emotional and mental filters when listening. Be aware of what a handshake tells you and how it may affect your listening.

Gestures Exercise #2

Directions: Have another person give the gesture for each of the following verbals. Write down what you think that person is communicating. Then switch roles.

"Stop!"

"Come here!"

"Shhh..."

"The fish that got away was this big."

"Are you hungry?"

"It's okay!"

"Good job!"

"The second point is..."

Other gestures that are used for communication:

Remember These Tips When Using Gestures to Communicate:

- Sitting or standing up straight sends the message that you are listening. Slouching sends the message that you are not interested.

- Avoid crossed arms and legs. These give the message that your mind is made up on the subject, that you disagree, that you're trapped or that you are stubborn.

- Avoid restless movement. It signals that you are bored.

- Avoid nervous gestures such as tapping your pen or bouncing your leg up and down. This can indicate that you are bored or nervous. It is also distracting to others who are trying to listen. Being aware of nervous gestures will allow you to control them. Sometimes you can channel the nervousness into other activities, such as doodling. You also may want to try some relaxation techniques such as deep breathing.

Nervous Gestures That I Can Control

Directions: List nervous gestures that you use regularly. Then indicate how you could control them.

Gesture	How to Control
Tapping pencil on table	*Tap pencil on my leg under the table*

- Mirror the speaker's body language. This indicates that you agree with what he is saying. If he assumes a relaxed posture, so should you. Most people will do this unconsciously. If you are in agreement with the speaker, you tend to mirror his body language. If the person who is speaking to you crosses his arms and you also cross your arms, you are mirroring him. As in a mirror, quite often, the gesture will be reversed—his right arm over his left and your left arm over your right.

- If you aren't sure what a gesture means, but you think it is crucial to understanding what the sender is trying to communicate, ask for clarification.

- Use gestures to emphasize rather than sending your whole message. For example, hold up three fingers as you say, "Point number three is..."

• **Posture**

While gesturing involves communicating with one part of your body, posture involves your whole body. It gives a speaker an overall impression of what you think as a listener.

Case Study:

You arrive at the meeting a few minutes early, take your place and observe your co-workers. Larry is slumped over in his chair, chin leaning on his hands. Margaret is sitting upright, almost at precise angles, adjusting her notebook. May is sitting comfortably in the chair, arms at her side, a slight smile on her face. Ted is pacing back and forth at the back of the room, looking up at every little noise. Each of them is communicating through his or her posture.

Case Study Analysis:

Larry is communicating fatigue and worry, while Margaret is communicating an overly businesslike attitude. May is communicating that she is ready and comfortable with the situation, while Ted is communicating nervousness and agitation.

**C
A
S
E

S
T
U
D
Y**

Follow These Two Techniques to Assess Posture and What It Communicates:

- Look for the big picture when assessing posture. Do not worry about the details such as eyebrows.

- Be aware that the person's posture may communicate the opposite of his words. His posture may look like he is not interested because he appears to be sitting back, relaxed, when, in fact, he is in a I'm-thinking-seriously-about-what-you-just-said mode.

• **Eye Contact**

One of the cardinal rules of speaking to a group is to maintain eye contact. Without eye contact, the speaker conveys to the group that he doesn't care about them or the subject. Eye contact is essential in communication. Talking to someone who is wearing dark glasses, for example, affects your communication. If you're like most people, you find dark glasses frustrating because you can't fully assess what the person is communicating. And because you can't see his eyes, you don't know if he is really listening to you.

Use These Techniques for Assessing Eye Contact:

- Maintain eye contact with the person or persons you are speaking or listening to.

- Be aware that the speaker in a one-on-one conversation will have more eye contact than the listener. It is normal for the listener to occasionally look away.

- Be aware that the eyes, eyelids, eyebrows and forehead can convey subtle messages. For example, there is a big difference between eyes that are squinted in concentration with the forehead furrowed and eyes that are wide open with the eyebrows raised. The first communicates confusion, the second surprise. Learning to read those subtleties will make you a better listener.

- Place yourself directly across from the person you are listening to for the best eye contact.

• **Vocal Cues**

Vocal cues comprise 35 percent of how we communicate. Instead of telling someone to choose his words carefully, the advice should be, "Choose the way you say your words carefully." It's possible, for example, to know when a speaker on the phone is smiling just from the vocal cues. Each of us has heard this saying at one time or another:

> ## "It's not what you say, it's how you say it."

There Are Four Kinds of Vocal Cues:

- **Pitch** — the highness or lowness of your voice. Pitch is genetically determined. However, nervousness can cause a person to speak in a much higher pitched voice than usual. Listening for pitch can help you assess what the speaker means.

- **Rate** — how fast or slowly you talk. In some cases, rate varies regionally. For example, people who live in rural areas tend to speak slower than those who live in cities. Similarly, people who live in the South have a slower speaking rate than those who live elsewhere. Rate may also vary depending on a person's emotions. Someone who is nervous or excited will speak more rapidly than normal.

- **Volume** — the loudness or softness of your voice. Each person has a volume that is normal for him in everyday situations. A person's speaking volume is sometimes related to self-image. Boastful people quite often speak loudly to disguise their poor self-esteem. Poor self-esteem also may cause a person to be soft-spoken, afraid that he or she might be heard. Unfortunately, some people think that the louder they speak, the easier it is for others to understand them. Understanding should not be equated with volume.

"Don't look at me, Sir, with-ah-in that tone of voice."

Punch

- **Quality** — the actual sound of your voice. Unless you take voice lessons, you can probably do little about your voice quality. Deep, resonating voices often are heard but not listened to effectively. Nasal, raspy or whiny voices often give a negative impression and may be difficult to listen to.

My Vocal Cues Assessment

Directions: Describe your own vocal cues below. Then indicate how your vocal cues affect people listening to you. Finally, list ways you can improve your vocal cues so people will listen to you more effectively.

Pitch:

Rate:

Volume:

Quality:

Ways my vocal cues affect listening to me:

In addition to the four vocal cues, the emphasis that you place on individual words can make a big difference in your communication.

Emphasis Practice

Directions: Practice saying the following sentence, emphasizing the underlined word in each line. How has the emphasis changed the meaning of what is communicated in each line?

Sentence	Meaning
<u>I</u> do not want a raise today.	*Others may, but not me*
I <u>do</u> not want a raise today.	
I do <u>not</u> want a raise today.	
I do not <u>want</u> a raise today.	
I do not want <u>a</u> raise today.	
I do not want a <u>raise</u> today.	
I do not want a raise <u>today.</u>	

"*Communication is something so simple and difficult that we can never put it in simple words.*"

T. S. Matthews

Practice These Techniques to Be a Better Listener of Vocal Cues:

- Listen for the intent of the speaker. The nonverbal vocal cues communicate the intent. The words may say something entirely different. For example, there's a big difference between saying, "Isn't that nice," sarcastically or sincerely.

- Respond to confusing signals with "I" messages. For example, "I understand you to say that..." or "The message I'm getting is... ." "I" messages are nonjudgmental and allow for further communication.

- Cue in on the pitch, rate and volume of the speaker. This will help you understand his emotional state. For example, if the speaker is talking more rapidly, higher and louder than usual, he is probably nervous.

- Listen carefully despite the poor quality of the speaker's voice. He can do little about it without professional help. You may have to listen extra carefully to his words, so be patient.

- Be aware of your own vocal cues when responding. Remember, for the most part, it's not what you say that people hear, it's how you say it. The best speech in the world can be ignored if it is delivered poorly.

- **Appearances**

A commercial on television says you have only one chance to make a good first impression. Much as we may not like to believe it, appearances do count and they do communicate. If they didn't, books such as *Dress for Success* wouldn't have been best-sellers. As a society, we seem constantly to be walking a tightrope between dressing like everyone else so that we can belong and dressing for ourselves so that we can be individuals.

Does the firm you work for have a written or unwritten dress code? If it does have a written dress code, how do people dress within the code and still express their individuality? Usually it's through use of jewelry, ties, scarves, hairstyle, mustaches and quality of clothing.

If your business doesn't have a written dress code, it probably has an understood or unstated one. Is there anyone at work who consistently dresses at the limit or out of the implied code? What is he communicating? Freedom? Individuality? Rebellion?

> *"Keep up appearances whatever you do."*
>
> *Charles Dickens*

My Business Dress Code

Directions: Whether written or unwritten, state the dress code where you work:

Response:

Dress Code Assessment

Directions: Assess how your co-workers dress within the code and what their clothing communicates.

Co-Worker:

Co-Worker Dress within Code:

What Clothing Communicates:

Use These Techniques for Listening to Appearance Communication

- Is the speaker's message influenced by your perception of his appearance? For example, do you automatically not listen to someone who is short or someone who wears flashy jewelry?

- Assess what you are communicating with your own appearance. How can you change your appearance if you are unhappy with it?

How My Appearance Affects How Others Listen to Me

Directions: List those things that you could change about your appearance that would change the way people listen to you.

	Change	Perception
1.	*New hairstyle*	*Up-to-date, fresh*
2.		
3.		
4.		
5.		

- Does the sender's appearance unduly distract you and cause you to ignore his communication? If so, try to overlook his appearance and focus on what he is saying. If his rumpled clothes bother you, concentrate on his face and maintain eye contact.

- When communicating, stick to the subject. Don't comment on the appearance of the person you are communicating with during the discussion. For example, don't say, "My that's a nice tie," or "Where did you get your bracelet?"

• Personal Space

Each culture has unspoken rules governing how close people can come to each other before they feel uncomfortable. Your use of personal space communicates to the people around you. Americans usually feel most comfortable when their personal space is not invaded. Personal space acts like an invisible barrier that stretches about 2 feet out from each person. In actuality, anthropologists define Americans' space in four different ways.

Intimate: Up to 1 1/2 feet away. This type is used for intimate conversations, hugging, sharing secrets and holding babies.

Personal: 1 1/2 to 4 feet away. This type is used for quiet conversation, one-to-one conversation and small-group interaction. It is the type we use the most and feel the most comfortable with.

Social: 4 to 12 feet away. This type is used for group discussions and parties.

Public: More than 12 feet away. This type is used for giving a speech or communicating over a distance, such as calling out or waving to someone.

When our personal space of 2 feet is invaded, such as in crowds or in elevators, Americans tend to create a psychological personal space and avoid eye contact. We feel uncomfortable being so close to a stranger, so in a sense we shut them out. Out of sight, out of mind.

> *"Personal space refers to an area with invisible boundaries surrounding a person's body into which intruders may not come."*
>
> *Robert Sommer*

"Let there be spaces in your togetherness."

Kahlil Gibran

In most business meetings, personal space has already been determined. Chairs are set up at a "respectable" distance, and a podium separates the speaker and audience. However, there are situations in which personal space affects communication.

- Movement toward a person that invades his personal space is usually seen as aggressive.

- Neutral touching, such as a pat on the back, is seen by some as positive. For others, touching even in a neutral or forbidden zone is interpreted as sexual. Even an innocent pat on the back can lead to a sexual-harassment suit.

- Placing an object between you and another person creates both a physical and psychological barrier. For example, a podium distances the speaker from his audience, giving him something to "hide" behind. A stack of two or three notebooks has the same effect when placed on a table.

- Leaning forward in your chair will send the message that you are interested in what the speaker has to say. It is an active listening space.

- Moving your chair back may send the message that you have distanced yourself. For others, it is a psychological distancing necessary for thought.

Summary

It is important that you monitor your response to the speaker, both nonverbally and verbally. If you don't, the speaker will get the impression that you are not listening. When that happens, you are setting up barriers to future communication. If the speaker feels you are actively listening, he is more likely to listen to you. It is important to complete the communication loop from speaker to listener and back to speaker.

Review Questions:

1. What are the various types of nonverbal communication?

2. How does nonverbal communication affect your listening?

3. What nonverbal communication can you control so that others can listen to you more effectively?

4. What techniques can you use immediately to improve your ability to listen to nonverbal communication?

CHAPTER 7

Getting Poor Listeners to Listen to You

Hearing is easy. Listening is hard. Listening requires a concentrated effort on the part of the receiver to understand what is being said as well as to interpret the body language of the sender. Hearing, on the other hand, is simply hearing what is said. For example, you can "listen" to an entire Italian opera and not understand because it was in a foreign language. You have **heard** the opera. You have not **listened** to it. Foreign languages are an extreme example of hearing but not understanding. At one time or another, all of us have even heard English words and phrases and not had any idea what they meant. Even if you are practicing Active or Reflective Listening, it doesn't mean that others will make the effort to listen to you as well as you are listening to them. Frustration with others' inability to listen can eventually get in the way of your effective listening skills.

1. **Give a recent example of a time when you heard something that you didn't understand. Why didn't you understand?**

2. **Give a recent example of a time when you said something that was heard but not understood. Why weren't you understood?**

> *"While seeing they do not see, and while hearing they do not hear, nor do they understand."*
>
> *Jesus*
> *(Matthew 11:13)*

103

One of the reasons people are sometimes heard but not understood is the language they've used. Look at the following levels of language that sometimes cause miscommunication:

Obscenities:	Unacceptable language by community standards
Slang:	Informal, faddish terms used for a short period of time
Technical language:	Language specific to a particular profession or job
Cultural or ethnic terms:	Terms used primarily by a cultural or ethnic group
Regional dialect:	Terms used only in a particular geographic area
Substandard English:	Grammatically incorrect language or misuse of words
Standard English:	Language taught in the schools as "correct"
Formal or academic English:	Language featuring a large vocabulary

You may find each of these levels of language used in your business and some of them in your personal life.

• **Obscenities**

Even the Supreme Court has trouble defining what is obscene and what is not. For the listener, obscene is what he thinks is obscene, regardless of whether it sounds that way to the speaker. You probably know an older family member who won't let you say "darn" because he thinks it is obscene. At the same time, that relative may use an expression such as "horsefeathers" with tremendous venom. Even though he doesn't see "horsefeathers" as obscene, that is the clear message he is sending. Knowing a person's background will help you know what is appropriate or inappropriate when using words that might be classified as swearing or obscene.

1. **How has your own background affected your ability to listen to obscenities?**

Obscene language can completely turn the receiver off from listening to what the sender says. It is important to be aware of what you are saying and how it affects others.

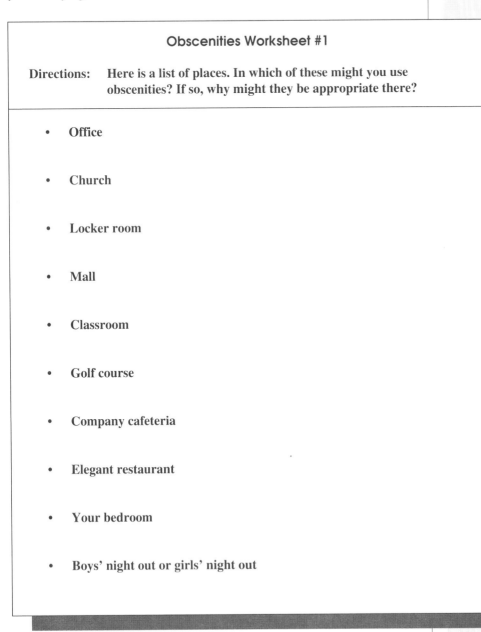

Obscenities Worksheet #1

Directions: Here is a list of places. In which of these might you use obscenities? If so, why might they be appropriate there?

- **Office**

- **Church**

- **Locker room**

- **Mall**

- **Classroom**

- **Golf course**

- **Company cafeteria**

- **Elegant restaurant**

- **Your bedroom**

- **Boys' night out or girls' night out**

Isn't it interesting how the place you're in affects your language? Compare your answers with those of your co-workers, your spouse and your teenager, and you may find some surprises. For some people, obscenities are simply not acceptable any place. For others, they are acceptable in certain places or situations.

Obscenities Worksheet #2

Directions: **Look at this list of people. Indicate with whom you could use obscenities while keeping communication open. Indicate with whom the use of an obscenity would close down communication.**

Spouse

Boyfriend

Girlfriend

Boss

Best friend

Minister/priest/rabbi

Mother

Son/daughter

Person you manage

Father

Waiter/waitress

With some you may not be sure, but with others you have no doubt!

When use of obscenities comes up, follow these guidelines:

- If you are offended by the obscenity, politely tell the speaker.

- If you do not know the speaker, try to ignore the obscenity unless it offends you so much that you can't.

- Be aware of the effect your own "acceptable" obscenities may have on the listener.

- Remember that some people use obscenities as a way to emphasize a point or to get your attention.

- Remember that different types of obscenities offend different types of people. For example, many older people will accept obscenities that were used during their youth but are offended by obscenities used today. Other people are offended mostly by obscenities using the name of God or obscenities dealing with bodily functions.

- Remember, in spite of women's liberation a double standard in terms of language still remains. In particular, many older people think it's inappropriate to swear in front of women.

- The easy solution to the obscenity problem is to avoid using any.

> *"Slang is a language that rolls up its sleeves, spits on its hand and goes to work."*
>
> *Carl Sandburg*

- **Slang**

In many ways, slang has an effect similar to obscenities. Slang can turn some people completely off, while getting little reaction from others. Slang is informal, nonstandard vocabulary. Usually, it is unique to a group and faddish, that is, it doesn't last more than three to five years. On occasion, a slang term will enter the language and stay.

In the business world, you are likely to use and encounter slang because it is very much a part of our everyday language. Because of the mass media — television and radio — large audiences are introduced to slang terms. Consequently, all of us use slang on a regular basis.

Slang Worksheet

Directions: List below 10 slang terms that you use today, but that you didn't use when you were younger. Then list the equivalent slang term from your adolescent years. Place check marks beside those slang terms that you think may be misunderstood by your co-workers.

Term Used Today	Term Used in My Adolescence
1. *Ticked off*	1. *Hacked off*
2.	2.
3.	3.
4.	4.
5.	5.
6.	6.
7.	7.
8.	8.
9.	9.
10.	10.

Here are some guidelines to using slang in communication.

- the use of slang in informal communication will seem natural.

- the use of slang in formal communication, such as a business meeting, a business letter or contact with a client, will seem artificial.

- If you're listening to a person using slang and you don't understand what he is saying, ask him to clarify.

- If you are "turned off" by slang, try to ignore the slang and listen for the intent of the sender.

- **Technical Language**

Technical language will be less of a problem at work than it will be somewhere else. Technical language, sometimes called jargon, is the language or terms you use for your work or area of specialization. However, it does not have to be work-related. It can include terms used for a particular sport or field of study.

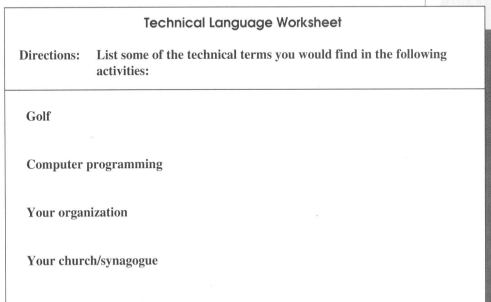

Technical Language Worksheet

Directions: List some of the technical terms you would find in the following activities:

Golf

Computer programming

Your organization

Your church/synagogue

The list is endless. The problems with technical language stem from communication between someone who is familiar with the technical language and someone who is not. For example, a client may have difficulty understanding your technical language even though he is more than willing to use your product. Remember, when you take your work home in the evening and talk in your company's technical language, you might as well be speaking French to your family. Keep the technical language to yourself unless you're talking to someone who's as well-versed as you are.

Here are some suggestions of how to use technical language in communication.

- Ask the sender to put the technical language into everyday terms if you don't understand what he is saying.

- If the sender uses technical language occasionally, try to understand it from the context or the way he uses it.

- Keep your technical language to a minimum when speaking with someone who doesn't use it.

- Don't assume the receiver understands technical language. Analyze his body language and listen carefully for verbal clues that indicate his level of understanding.

How does technical language impede your own communication?

When have you been a listening victim of technical language?

"I want no more than to speak simply, to be granted that grace ..."

George Seferis

- **Cultural/Ethnic Terms**

Each of us comes from a particular culture or ethnic background —
perhaps a very strong one. When you communicate, you are likely
to use some of the language of your youth or your culture. Cultural
or ethnic terms are more likely to cause communication problems in
informal or social situations than in business meetings. Usually, the
more education you have, the more standardized your vocabulary.
Standard English is essentially the language of business. However,
around the water cooler, cultural terms may cause a lack of
understanding.

Example:

In my hometown, everyone would understand if something is
verboten (forbidden) because it is a German-American
community. In my wife's hometown, people are perfectly
comfortable ordering potatis korv (potato bologna) from the
butcher because it is a Swedish-American community. Our
Jewish friends talk of the High Holidays (religious holidays). In
the town where I live kolaches (Czech pastries) and baklava
(Greek pastries) are common words because of the Czech-
American and Greek-American influences. These are all
cultural or ethnic terms.

Cultural/Ethnic Worksheet

Directions: List below the cultural or ethnic terms that people who do not have
your background may have trouble understanding. Then list terms
that your co-workers use that you have trouble understanding.

Terms I Use	**Terms My Co-Workers Use**
Year of the Sheep (Chinese)	*Cinco de Mayo (Mexican)*

Here are some techniques to use when confronted with cultural or ethnic language difficulties.

- Smile and ask for a clarification of the term used.

- Take a genuine interest in the culture or ethnic background of the speaker or listener. You may find it quite different, but there will probably be many points of similarity.

- Be aware of your own cultural or ethnic terminology. This may be difficult because it is so much a part of you and because everyone around you uses it.

• Regional Dialects

Regional dialects are those words, expressions and accents that are used in a specific region of the country. Because of television and radio, many of the regional variations no longer exist, but the media have not completely erased all of them. In the South, Midwest, Brooklyn, New Jersey, and the Valley area of California and Texas regional languages still exist. To some extent, everyone has an accent and a dialect and uses regional language. If you live in the Midwest, you may not think this is true because the media have adopted the Midwestern accent as their standard.

Regional terminology will become a communication problem only if you move to a different region than the one you grew up in or if someone from another region moves to your hometown. In other words, thanks to our mobile society, you will probably run into regional terminology. While cultural or ethnic language tends to be used in informal or social situations, regional terminology may also be found in business environments. Once again, education erases many of the regionalisms, but not all. For example, parts of the country call the receptacle you carry groceries in a "bag" while others call it a "sack." In some areas asking for a coke will get you a blank look because coke is generic for soft drink. In other areas you will get a Coke®. You should have asked for "soda," "soda pop" or "pop." In some places people drink from a "water fountain," while in others they drink from a "bubbler."

> *"It takes a great man to make a good listener."*
>
> *Sir Arthur Helps*

Here are some guidelines to help in dealing with regional language.

- Ask the speaker where he is from if he uses terminology that is obviously not cultural or technical.

- Politely ask him to explain terms you don't understand.

- Put aside your own prejudices when it comes to accents. The speaker would have as much difficulty changing his accent as you would yours. Empathize with him.

- Be aware of your own regionalisms and accent. Read the listener's body language so that you know how you are affecting him.

- If you are new to a region, make a "dictionary" of regional terminology to study.

- When using a regional term the first few times, don't assume that your usage is correct. The saying "When in Rome, do as the Romans," doesn't always apply to speaking.

• **Substandard, Standard and Formal or Academic**

Do you remember when your high school English teacher said, "Don't use 'ain't'. 'Ain't' isn't a word," and you sat smugly in your chair with the knowledge that 'ain't' was in the dictionary? What the teacher was trying to explain was the difference between standard and nonstandard English.

Key Idea:

> The business world uses standard English. The everyday, informal world outside of business uses a combination of standard and nonstandard English. It is sprinkled with slang, regional terminology, cultural and ethnic terms and obscenities. Formal or academic language builds on standard English but uses a larger vocabulary.

Here Are Some Examples of the Differences Among Substandard, Standard and Formal or Academic English

Substandard:	He don't go there no more.
Standard:	He doesn't go there anymore.
Formal or Academic:	He no longer goes there.

Substandard:	I ain't got no time for them stinkin' cops.
Standard:	I don't have any time for those awful police.
Formal or Academic:	I have no time for those dastardly police officers.

Substandard English relies heavily on the misuse of grammar and language. Standard English is the "correct" form taught in school. Formal or academic English is standard English with the addition of a larger vocabulary. It is also the language of formal written documents and is not usually spoken.

"Naturally I am biased in favor of boys learning English; I would make them all learn English: and then I would let the clever ones learn Latin as an honor, and Greek as a treat."

Sir Winston Churchill

Our society associates the inability to use standard English with a lack of education. Unfortunately, once you open your mouth your language gives you away. In many cases, regional or cultural language relies heavily on nonstandard English, thus complicating the problem of communication even more.

Follow these techniques when listening to different levels of language.

- Be aware that the language of business is standard English.

- Be sensitive, however, to the person who uses substandard English. His ideas may be perfectly valid even though his English is not "correct."

- Keep an open mind when listening to someone who uses substandard English.

- Keep an open mind when listening to someone who uses formal or academic English. He may not be putting on airs or be a stuffed shirt. It may be natural speech for him.

- If you use substandard English, identify your misuses and try to correct yourself, at least within the business world.

"The foolish and the dead alone never change their opinion."

James Russell Lowell

Uses of Language

When we communicate using other than standard English, we do so for three main reasons:

- To make the listener part of our group or to exclude him. For example, if you are in management, you may choose to use less than perfect English with those you supervise if it will make them more comfortable. In the same situation, you could use perfect English to make your subordinates feel excluded.

- To make the listener feel good about himself or to put him down. Using the same level of language as the listener will make him feel good about himself because it sends the message that you accept him. Using a pretentious level of language can make the listener feel inferior if that is not his normal level of language.

- To reveal or conceal ourselves. Sometimes people put on airs through their language to cover up their "roots." At other times people's childhood "roots" sneak out when they use their childhood language.

These uses can be accomplished through the use of substandard English, formal or academic English, regional or cultural speech, slang or obscenities — any type of language that is not standard.

**Follow the Rule of Thumb concerning
language and communication:
Know your audience. Know yourself. Adjust accordingly.**

Getting a Poor Listener to Understand What You Are Saying

It's not enough that you have to be concerned about what people are saying and what they are hearing. You must also be concerned about how to get them to listen to you so they can understand what you are saying.

How can you get people to listen to you more effectively?

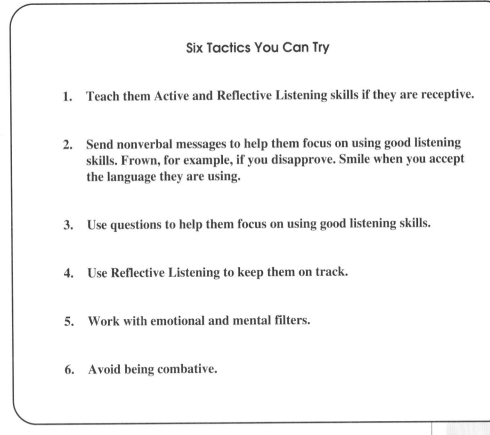

Six Tactics You Can Try

1. Teach them Active and Reflective Listening skills if they are receptive.

2. Send nonverbal messages to help them focus on using good listening skills. Frown, for example, if you disapprove. Smile when you accept the language they are using.

3. Use questions to help them focus on using good listening skills.

4. Use Reflective Listening to keep them on track.

5. Work with emotional and mental filters.

6. Avoid being combative.

Each of these tactics will help other people to start focusing on good listening skills. Depending on the situation, you may want to use all or just one of the tactics. Let's look at each one closely.

> # Tactic # 1:
> ## Teach Them Active and Reflective Listening Skills If They Are Receptive

In some business and personal situations you can teach or provide direction so others can acquire good listening skills. In business, these situations could include instructing subordinates or assisting co-workers. In personal situations, you can help your children, spouse or close friends become better listeners. Whatever the case, those involved initially have to understand the benefits of good listening.

If your "audience" is receptive, suggest they learn about effective listening skills through seminars, books or by talking with you. Explain the importance of effective listening. If you feel confident about your understanding of effective listening skills, explain the basics of Active and Reflective Listening and then encourage them to study further.

How will you know if your audience is ready to learn more about listening? Here are a few clues.

- If you are complimented on your good listening skills, use it as an opportunity to suggest ways the person giving the compliment could learn more about listening.

- If you have recently learned about effective listening skills through a seminar or book and your co-workers or family know this, informally share what you have learned.

- When someone asks you how you became such a good listener, explain what you did.

- When a group you are working with is frustrated and you know it is because of poor listening, suggest ways to eliminate the frustrations by using effective listening skills.

> ## Tactic # 2:
> ## Send Nonverbal Messages to Help Them Focus on Using Good Listening Skills

When people are not receptive to learning more about effective listening skills, you need to use a more subtle approach. Send a nonverbal message that they are responding inappropriately to what you have said. Your message should say, "Get back on track," or "You're not listening to me."

Here are some examples of nonverbal signals that can be used.

- Look puzzled when they respond. Make your expression convey that they haven't understood what you said.

- Frown if you disapprove of their response because they have not heard what you said. This is not meant to be a judgmental response to their ideas. It is a response to their Inactive or Selective Listening.

"What we've got here is a failure to communicate."

"Cool Hand Luke"
Screenplay, 1967

- Take notes on their response. When coupled with a verbal response from you, note-taking can send the message that they are accountable for what's being said.

- Move forward to show that you are listening. Combine this with facial expressions indicating that you don't understand why they responded the way they did.

- Lean back in your chair and take a "I'm-thinking-about-what-you're-saying" pose. Then respond verbally and discuss how they didn't listen to what you were saying.

You can only go so far when dealing with a poor listener on a nonverbal level. Remember, your nonverbal cues may be ignored or misinterpreted. If you don't get the desired response, combine your nonverbal messages with verbal communication.

Tactic # 3:

Use Questions to Help Them Focus on Using Good Listening Skills

---

A very effective way to get poor listeners to practice good listening skills is to pose questions that require them to think about the point that you were trying to make. The questions may be either open-ended or closed-ended depending on the situation.

Examine the following case-study dialogue between co-workers. Notice that Jack does not hear Louis' response, so Louis uses questions to get Jack to focus on what Louis said.

Case Study:

Jack: Well, I'm all ready to head home.

Louis: Great. Don't forget to be here an hour earlier tomorrow. We've got to get a good start on the Davis house. Did you take the specs along to look at tonight?

C A S E   S T U D Y

Jack: Yeah, sure. Big evening ahead. Mona and Sam are coming over.

Louis: Are you going to be able to look at the specs tonight?

Jack: Oh, yeah, sure. They're not coming until 8 o'clock. I'll go over them as soon as I get home.

Louis: That's good because you really need to know what you're doing tomorrow. Will they be there late?

Jack: Gee, I don't know.

Louis: Do they usually stay late?

Jack: No, they're usually gone by eleven.

Louis: Then you shouldn't have any trouble getting here an hour earlier?

Jack: No problem.

Louis: Good. I'll see you tomorrow. You want me to call you in the morning?

Jack: That's not a bad idea. Would you?

Louis: Sure. See you tomorrow.

Case Study Questions:

1. What type of questions did Louis use to get Jack to focus?

2. How did the questions keep Jack on track?

In this case, closed-ended questions were asked. There was only one possible answer to each of them. The questions helped Jack focus on what he had not heard: the time of the curfew and the reason for the curfew.

C A S E   S T U D Y

In some situations, open-ended questions may work better.

Case Study:

During a business meeting you suggest that the Sales and Marketing Division be split into two separate divisions so each can focus on what it does best. In the subsequent discussion it becomes apparent that your audience has heard only that the Sales and Marketing Division should be split. The audience members have not heard your reasons for the split. Open-ended questions such as "What are some of the advantages of such a split?" or "How would a split allow the company to increase profits?" would help the audience focus on your reasons.

Case Study Questions:

1. How would you know if your audience had not heard your entire message?

2. What other open-ended questions could you use to help your audience focus on the reasons for the split?

3. Could closed-ended questions be used?

4. If so, in what way?

- Open-ended questions are general. They can help clarify issues that the listener hasn't heard. They need to be phrased so that they lead the listener to think about what they didn't hear.

- Closed-ended questions are specific and ask the listener about what you have just said.

Key Idea:

Open-ended questions can be used in almost any situation. Closed-ended questions may be misinterpreted as being assertive, aggressive or combative and should be used carefully. Closed-ended questions tend to put the listener on the defensive.

Important Tip:

A manager can use closed-ended questions with his employees more effectively than an employee can use them with his manager. Closed-ended questions indicate control or superiority.

Tactic # 4:
Use Reflective Listening to Keep Others on Track

Another tactic to get someone to listen is to use Reflective Listening. This is particularly effective in a one-on-one situation or when you have sufficient time. Reflective Listening also can be used occasionally in group communication although it is more difficult. For twice the impact on poor listeners, combine questions with Reflective Listening.

To a poor listener, Reflective Listening responses work this way: "I hear you saying... Did you hear me saying...?" You tell him what you heard, then you ask him what he heard. This forces him to examine his poor listening skills.

Following are responses that you can use to get a poor listener to focus on what you are saying.

- "When you said..., did you mean...?" This can be used to connect what he heard to what you said.

- "Do I understand you to say...?"

- "I understand your point." (Then explain the point). "I wonder if you understood my point." (Then explain your point.)

- "Let's look at what you said compared to what I said."

- "I wonder if you understood what I said." Then repeat what you said earlier.

Reflective Listening Response Practice

Directions: Write a response that uses Reflective Listening for the following situations:

Example #1:

In a one-on-one meeting with your boss, you tell her that there is a potential problem in shipping that could lead to a strike. The situation has been caused by a misinterpretation in a recent policy she issued. Her response is "Oh, it's nothing. The union will get over it." But you know that this is not the case.

Reflective Listening Response: *"When you said, 'It's nothing,' did you mean that there'll be no consequences to this problem?"*

Example #2:

When ordering a new shipment of office equipment you have the following phone conversation with the office-equipment supplier:

You: "The last time that we ordered equipment from your company, it was back-ordered for six months. That was the first time that we ever had this problem with you. Will there be any problem in getting this order here by next month?"

Supplier: "I always say, 'it'll get there when it gets there.' "

Reflective Listening Response:

Example #3:

A co-worker tells you that he is having trouble with another co-worker in getting part of a joint project finished on time. The man who is dragging his feet seems to be preoccupied. Your perception is that the two of them have been having trouble communicating. You realize that the co-worker dragging his feet is doing it just to get back at the other. The co-worker telling you about the problem doesn't hear you saying this. He just wants to blame the other guy.

Reflective Listening Response:

Summary:

Using Reflective Listening can be effective because it acknowledges the other person but always comes back to what you originally said. It forces the poor listener to hear your message a second time.

"The best part of human language, properly so called, is derived from reflection on the acts of the mind itself."

Samuel Taylor Coleridge

Tactic # 5:
Work with Emotional and Mental Filters

If you know your listener well, you can use his emotional or mental filters to get him to listen. This is done by phrasing what you have to say so that his filters will work for you rather than against you. Salespeople and politicians have used this technique for years. It is the fine art of finding the "hot buttons" that make a person want to listen to what you have to say.

Use this technique when you know your listener well and can speak his language.

Case Study Analysis:

Let's examine the case study about splitting the Sales and Marketing Divisions. If you know that one of the major concerns about the split is job security, start your presentation by talking about how the change will affect employees' jobs, seniority and promotions. If possible, go on to discuss career opportunities that will be created. Like a debater, anticipate arguments and concerns that might result from your audience's emotional and mental filters.

C A S E   S T U D Y

?

Use These Techniques to Take Advantage of Your Listeners' Emotional and Mental Filters:

- If you have time, list the audience's concerns or emotional and mental filters about the topic to be discussed. Then list the ways that you can appeal to those concerns and filters.

- Also list what you think they do not want to hear or what they will filter out. Determine how you can present this information in a context that is acceptable.

Case Study:

You meet with Linda, Raoul and Germaine to go over staffing allotments. Linda thinks your boss, Ms. Tripp, can do no wrong. Raoul filters out anything negative about personnel because he once worked there. Germaine filters out anything that deals with layoffs because he doesn't want to face the possibility he might lose his job. The staffing allotments require that one person be laid off for the upcoming quarter. Using your knowledge of your co-workers' filters you start the meeting by saying, "Ms. Tripp talked to personnel concerning the staff allotments for next quarter. The good news is that no one at this meeting will lose his job. The bad news is that there will be one layoff in the division."

Case Study Questions:

1. How have you phrased what you said so that Linda will accept the allotments?

2. How have you phrased what you said so that Raoul will accept the allotments?

3. How have you phrased what you said so that Germaine will hear what you're talking about?

- If you don't have time to prepare, listen for verbal and nonverbal clues that indicate what your audience has heard and what they wanted to hear. Then respond. For example, heads nodding in agreement or positive comments help you cue into your audience's emotional and mental filters.

- Sometimes mirroring their nonverbals, such as body language, tone of voice or pace of speech, can help you communicate more clearly. For example, if the person you are talking to speaks slowly, slow your own speech down. If he is animated, become animated.

Mirroring Practice

Directions: Choose a situation in which you can mirror nonverbal communication and then analyze the response you have received.

Sample Situation Mirrored: *Talking to Jan, my secretary, who talks fast.*

Sample Response: *I talked faster than normal and she smiled like she understood what I was saying.*

Situation Mirrored:

Response:

Situation Mirrored:

Response:

Tactic # 6:
Avoid Being Combative

With some audiences you may become so frustrated that you want to argue.

Avoid arguing or becoming verbally combative at all costs.

This will only cause communication to break down even further. A good thing to remember is that it takes two to fight — one to start the fight and one to continue it.

Follow These Techniques to Avoid Arguments or Verbal Combats:

- Count to 10 instead of immediately responding.

- Ask yourself and others, "What is the issue we are discussing?"

- Use Reflective Listening to defuse the situation.

- Suggest a break in the discussion.

- List the key discussion points for all to see.

- Suggest that the agenda be followed.

- Say to yourself, "Whose problem is this?"

- Listen to what is being said and respond with empathy and without judging the speaker.

"Argument is the worst sort of conversation."

Jonathan Swift

- Use the tactics previously mentioned in this chapter.

- Refuse to enter into an argument. Just because someone starts a fight you don't have to continue it.

- Keep calm. Don't take the confrontation personally.

Case Study:

In your weekly managers' meeting, Matt, the head of Transportation, says, "I'm sick and tired of the way you guys in Accounting are always screwing up. Last week I found 10 mistakes that you jerks made. It's been going on like that for months now. What school did you go to? Goof-up U?" You are the newly appointed head of Accounting and are aware of the problems in your division.

Case Study Questions:

1. What techniques can you use to avoid getting into an argument with Matt?

2. What words has Matt used that make this a potentially combative situation?

3. What Reflective Listening statements can you use to help him identify the real problem?

4. What statements can you make that will defuse the situation but address the problem?

C
A
S
E

S
T
U
D
Y

Summary

Be a model of good listening to those around you. If you use Active Listening, eventually they will want to use it too. By trying some of the tactics in this chapter, you have nothing to lose and everything to gain.

My Action Plan for Getting Poor Listeners to Understand What I Am Saying

Directions: Fill in each of the boxes below.

My Action Plan:

Goals to Accomplish:

Obstacles Keeping Me from Accomplishing These Goals:

Steps to Accomplish These Goals:

Time line for Accomplishing These Goals:

Review Questions:

1. How can language affect the way you listen?

2. Of the various kinds of language listed at the beginning of this chapter, which are most likely to impede listening?

3. What are three tactics you can use to get a poor listener to listen to you?

4. How can you approach those who are receptive to learning about good listening skills?

5. How can you use nonverbal signals to get a poor listener to listen?

6. How can you use open-ended questions to get a poor listener to listen?

7. How can you use closed-ended questions to get a poor listener to listen?

8. With which type of co-worker would you most effectively use open-ended questions? Closed-ended questions?

9. How can you use emotional and mental filters to get a poor listener to listen to you?

10. Why is it important to avoid arguments or combative communication?

Using Listening to Minimize Conflicts

Active Listening can be used to minimize conflicts. Because you are assessing both verbal and nonverbal cues when you use Active Listening, you can keep conflicts to a minimum. Conflicts, like any fight, operate under the premise that it takes two to fight—one to start it and one to continue it. By using Active Listening, you avoid the conflict by not participating in it.

Characteristics of Verbal Conflicts

Here are some common characteristics of verbal conflicts:

- Verbal conflicts tend to be destructive rather than constructive. They tend to attack the person rather than the issue, which in turn damages the ego.

- Verbal conflicts tend to be emotional rather than logical. If they were logical they would be debates. Usually verbal conflicts deal with emotional issues.

- Verbal conflicts tend to be unfocused rather than focused. Because they are primarily emotional, they tend to ramble, jumping from one emotional issue to the next.

- Verbal conflicts tend to create problems rather than resolve them.

> *"Words are as beautiful as wild horses, and sometimes as difficult to corral."*
>
> *Ted Berkman*

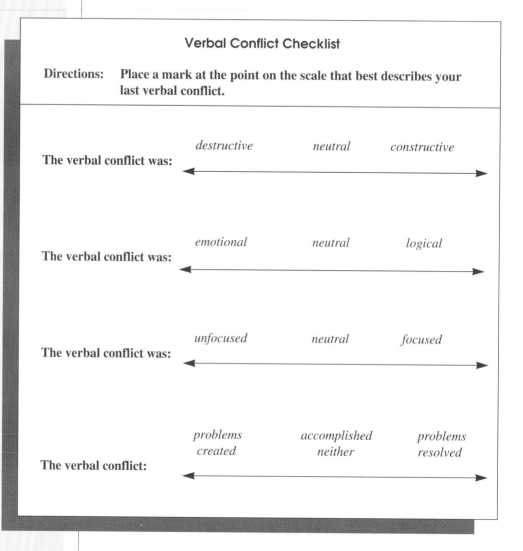

Verbal Conflict Checklist

Directions: Place a mark at the point on the scale that best describes your last verbal conflict.

The verbal conflict was:

destructive   *neutral*   *constructive*

The verbal conflict was:

emotional   *neutral*   *logical*

The verbal conflict was:

unfocused   *neutral*   *focused*

The verbal conflict:

*problems   accomplished   problems
created   neither   resolved*

In this chapter, we will explore listening techniques that help resolve a verbal conflict.

How Poor Listening Skills
Contribute to Arguments

Key Idea:

> Most arguments could be avoided if the participants used
> Active and Reflective Listening.

Most arguments start because one or both of the participants fail to
listen in an empathic and nonjudgmental way. The differences
between Active Listening (conflict-free) and Argumentative
Listening (conflict-invoking) are:

> **The Active Listener *listens* to the content.**
> **The Argumentative Listener *filters* the content.**

Key Idea:

> The Active Listener does not judge the content of what is said.
> If he is listening to a business presentation that uses facts and
> figures, he mentally or physically notes the content — facts,
> figures, words or ideas — and then, after getting the whole
> message, decides on a response.

Key Idea:

> The Argumentative Listener filters the same information,
> choosing the content that he agrees or disagrees with. Before
> getting the whole message, he forms a conclusion and a
> response, usually referring to the information he disagrees with.

Example:

Your manager says that production in your department is down 33 percent. The department is your direct responsibility. If you are an Active Listener, you will mentally note the figure and wait until you hear everything about the situation before you respond. If you are an Argumentative Listener, you will hear the words "down 33 percent" and immediately filter the rest of the message through your "excuse" filter, readying your argument for when your boss stops talking.

Listening-Situation Worksheet

Directions: List the situations in which you always listen to the content, those in which you are objective. Then list the situations in which you always filter the content, those in which you are subjective.

Situations in which I always listen to the content:	**Situations in which I always filter the content:**
When I listen to those I manage.	*When I listen to my performance review.*

Key Idea:

The Active Listener considers the intent of the speaker objectively and then responds to the whole message.

Key Idea:

The Argumentative Listener filters and judges the intent of the speaker's message and makes assumptions about both the speaker and the message. He bases his response, usually a rebuttal or argument, on his biased understanding of the speaker's intent.

> **The Active Listener *listens* to the intent.**
> **The Argumentative Listener *filters and judges* the intent.**

For instance, an Active Listener can identify various tactics used by a politician to trigger an emotional response from an audience. If a politician says, "Everybody agrees that raising taxes is a bad idea," the Active Listener will refrain from making a positive or negative judgment. However, he will be aware that the politician is using two emotional appeals. The first "everybody" is used to encourage jumping on the band wagon. In truth, there will be those who favor raising taxes. When the politician uses the word "everybody," he is appealing to your emotions and your desire to be like everybody else. The second emotional appeal is in the choice of words, "raising taxes is a bad idea." The word "bad" sends a red flag to the audience, who will likely want to disassociate itself from anything "bad." At the same time, an Argumentative Listener in the audience might react negatively by focusing on the politician's attempts to manipulate. He might argue with the politician instead of simply noting the faulty logic.

> *"There is no worse lie than a truth misunderstood by those who hear it."*
>
> *William James*

137

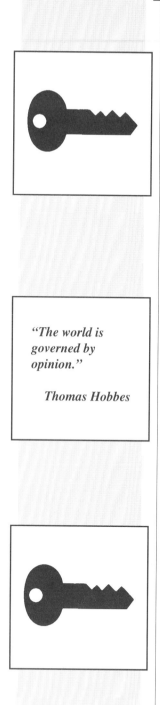

Key Idea:

The Active Listener uses the speaker's nonverbal communication to understand the complete message. For example, an Active Listener "reads" the speaker's nonverbal communication to understand what he is saying. If the speaker points his finger at the audience in a threatening manner, and says, "If we don't land the Bierbaum, Inc., contract, jobs will be lost," the Active Listener notes that the speaker is very concerned about the future of the company. He points his finger to emphasize his message.

Key Idea:

The Argumentative Listener reacts emotionally rather than intellectually to the speaker's nonverbal communication. In the previous example, the Argumentative Listener reacts by mentally arguing with the speaker or by perhaps becoming frightened at the prospect of losing his job.

The Active Listener
assesses **the speaker's nonverbal communication.**
The Argumentative Listener
reacts **to the speaker's nonverbal communication.**

Key Idea:

Because the Active Listener responds to the whole message, he is careful to control the nonverbal messages he sends to the speaker. He is also aware of his own emotional and mental filters. For example, he doesn't nod enthusiastically even though he may be in agreement with the speaker. To do so may be premature and prohibit a later discussion.

"The world is governed by opinion."

Thomas Hobbes

Key Idea:

The Argumentative Listener simply responds emotionally. He does not attempt to control his nonverbal communication or filters. His nonverbals allow him to be read like an open book. For example, his face gets red, he points his finger at you and he shouts—all telling you he is angry.

The Active Listener
monitors **his nonverbal communication and filters.**
The Argumentative Listener
ignores **his nonverbal communication and filters.**

Key Idea:

The Active Listener attempts to understand the speaker's position and message. He understands that listening in an empathic and nonjudgmental way keeps communication channels open. For example, if a co-worker says he is seriously considering early retirement because of the way management is treating him, the Active Listener will attempt to understand his position. He listens with empathy even though he may not agree that early-retirement action is in the best interest of his co-worker.

Key Idea:

The Argumentative Listener judges and evaluates the speaker according to his own standards and agenda. In the previous situation, the Argumentative Listener will judge and evaluate the co-worker's statement about early retirement. Depending on the Argumentative Listener's feelings, he may try to dissuade the co-worker or tell him to go ahead and pursue early retirement. The advice offered by the Argumentative Listener is based on his own standards, not on what is best for his co-worker.

> **The Active Listener**
> *listens* to the speaker with *empathy and nonjudgment*.
> **The Argumentative Listener**
> *judges and evaluates* the speaker.

If one person is using Active Listening and the other is not, a conflict may occur but it probably won't resolve anything. However, if both people use Active Listening, they may disagree with each other but they will still be able to communicate. They may even accomplish something!

Common Barriers to Effective Listening

Even though you use Active Listening, you are human. There will be times when the speaker says something that irritates you and you want to react emotionally. Part of your reaction may be triggered by one of five common barriers to effective listening.

Five Common Barriers to Effective Listening

- **Misreading nonverbals**

- **Hidden agenda**

- **Standards and expectations**

- **Prejudging**

- **Emotions vs. intellect**

Technique # 1:
Misreading nonverbals

It is easy to misread a nonverbal such as a smile or a frown. The speaker may be frowning because she is thinking of something, while you may think she is frowning at you. When you misread a nonverbal you get the wrong message. We often say, "Oh, she looked at you the wrong way." In other words, you probably misread the nonverbal message. Before you react or respond, take the whole message into consideration. If necessary, ask the speaker to clarify.

Example:

Sid is the shop supervisor for your department. He never smiles. To some, this means that Sid is never happy and he doesn't like their performance. To others, Sid's demeanor reflects their work ethic and efficiency. In both cases, Sid's workers need to listen to his verbal communication as well as his nonverbal communication to better understand him.

Technique # 2:
Hidden agendas

Each person has a hidden agenda — unspoken issues that relate to the conversation. Hidden agendas can lead to verbal conflict when they are not discussed openly or when one person feels so strongly that he or she cannot accept the other's position. Hidden agendas also cause conflict because they can produce a confusing or vague message.

Example:

Whenever Marlyse talks to her superiors, she manages to bring the conversation around to how little space her staff has. Obviously, her hidden agenda is to get a larger work area for her staff. Instead of just requesting the space in a logical manner, she uses each meeting to get her hidden agenda across. This angers her co-workers who are tired of hearing her complain.

> # Technique # 3:
> ## Standards and expectations

Similar to hidden agendas, standards and expectations can get in the way of Active Listening. If the speaker does not conform to the standards and expectations of the listener, the potential for verbal conflict increases greatly.

Example:

When Mark, a co-worker of yours, opens his mouth you can't listen objectively to him because his grammar and usage don't meet your standards. Even though his ideas are sound, you find yourself arguing with him because of the words he has chosen and how he has said them.

Standards and Expectations of People I Work with

Directions: List the standards and expectations of the people you work with regularly. Are those standards and expectations higher or lower than your own?

Person	Standards and Expectations
Bjorn	*Always expects me to use precise figures. If I don't, he won't listen.*

My Standards and Expectations

Directions: List your standards and expectations of the people you work with. How do they affect your ability to listen to them?

Example: *I expect people to come right to the point and not beat around the bush.*

Technique # 4:
Prejudging

If a person goes into a conversation having already prejudged the speaker, the groundwork has been laid for conflict. If you think your boss is unqualified and ineffective, naturally you are not going to listen to all that he says. If you are not going to listen, then you will probably disagree with something he says.

Example:

> You see your boss as unqualified for his job. If your boss says to you, "I think by moving Swartz to the Liaison Office we can better utilize his skills," you will probably think that he doesn't know anything about Swartz's abilities. You won't listen to what your boss says even though the move might be in the best interest of Swartz and the company. Prejudging will have gotten in the way of hearing your boss and will have clouded your judgment.

Prejudices That Affect My Listening

Directions: List below any prejudices that have affected your ability to listen objectively.

1. *I have trouble taking Southerners seriously.*

2.

3.

4.

5.

Prejudices That Affect How I Am Heard

Directions: List below any prejudices that may affect how people hear you.

1. *Listening to me as a woman in power.*

2.

3.

4.

5.

Technique # 5:
Emotions vs. intellect

All of these barriers are affected by your emotions. If you listen emotionally, you will encounter verbal conflicts because you will have read the speaker according to your emotional and mental filters. When you actively listen, you listen intuitively and intellectually, with your head rather than your heart.

Example:

Let's assume that someone you manage comes to you because he did not get a raise. He is visibly upset. He says that he was banking on the raise, so he had bought a new house. It was going to be really tight to make the payments without a raise. If you listen primarily with emotion, you will feel sorry for him and perhaps give him the raise. If you listen intellectually, you will hear that he has financially overextended himself. You will also remember that raises are based on work-performance criteria, not the needs of the worker. You should listen with empathy to what he says, but you probably shouldn't give him the raise based on his house payments.

Listening Techniques for Conflicts

Using Active Listening during an argument is the first step you can take to defuse the situation and solve whatever problems have arisen.

When people feel strongly about an issue, their emotions will color their ability to communicate and listen.

Example:

If you feel strongly that people are destroying the environment at an alarming rate, you will have more difficulty listening objectively to someone talk about environment-related issues. You may, for example, prejudge what he has to say. It is hard to listen objectively if you are emotionally involved. However, if you are going to make sound business decisions, you must suspend your emotions so that you can listen objectively to what is being said. In these situations, it is important to use a combination of Active and Reflective Listening skills. First, start with a Reflective Listening statement. This will show the speaker that you have heard what he said. Then respond to what he said.

Issues I Feel Strongly About That May Affect
My Ability to Communicate and Listen Effectively

Directions: List any issues or topics that you feel so strongly about that you have trouble listening to discussions about them.

1. *I have trouble listening to those who say "Buy American" in a global business climate.*

2.

3.

4.

5.

**Five Techniques to Defuse Conflicts
and Enhance Effective Communication**

- Criticize the issue or behavior, not the person.

- Remember that each person has worth.

- Avoid absolutes — right or wrong, bad or good.

- Send "I" messages or "I feel" messages.

- Engage your brain and suspend your emotions.

Technique # 1:
Criticize the issue or behavior, not the person.

By dealing with the issue or the behavior, you avoid attacking the other person. For example, if you are "arguing" with a co-worker about a late project, then stick to the issue of the lateness or to his behavior of being late. This is not the time to dredge up all of his past mistakes. These attack the person and damage his self-esteem, create barriers and probably do not correct the behavior. Instead, actively listen to what he has to say and keep him on track if he strays from the issue. Even if he does not use Active Listening, you must continue to do so. Your use of Active Listening will help defuse a potentially damaging situation.

Technique # 2:
Remember that each person has worth.

It is almost impossible to practice Active or Reflective Listening if you dismiss the speaker as inferior or worthless. You don't have to agree with him, but it is crucial that you respect his right to a different opinion and acknowledge his sense of value. Try to find something that the two of you have in common. Try to understand what the other person is saying and why he feels a certain way. Empathize with him, and you'll better understand his position.

Example:

> If you see your boss as ineffective and unqualified for his position, you may have trouble listening to what he says. You probably argue with him instead of discussing objectively those issues you disagree on. It would be helpful to identify your boss's positive points and to recognize what you have in common with him. For example, you may have graduated from the same college. Use that common bond to build a working relationship rather than an adversarial one.

Technique # 3:
Avoid absolutes — right or wrong, bad or good.

Statements like "you always" or "you never" are absolutes. They are sweeping generalizations that impede communication. An Active Listener will pick up on these right away and counter with a statement such as "I hear you saying I always favor those people I hire, but in actuality I...." Statements that categorize someone or something as right-wrong or bad-good also impede communication.

This is not to say there aren't situations or people that are definitely right or wrong or bad or good. However, in an argument, the truth is usually somewhere in between. Sweeping generalizations polarize a conflict. The focus shifts from solving the problem at hand to each person effectively arguing his position.

"Worth makes the man ..."

Alexander Pope

> *"I have often regretted my speech; never my silence."*
>
> ***Publilius Syrus***

Example:

You are in charge of the company newsletter. Bill, a division chair, complains to you that his division has not received enough recognition. When you ask his division to submit material, they don't respond 85 percent of the time. You also know that Bill's division is understaffed. If you are not an Active Listener, it would be very easy to respond to his initial complaint with, "Your guys never hand anything in." That statement would be an absolute. However, it would not be true, because occasionally they do hand in material. An absolute statement would only cause a verbal conflict with Bill.

Technique # 4:
Send "I" messages or "I feel" messages.

"I" messages tell the speaker how you feel about what he is saying. They are different from "you" messages. "You" messages put words into the other person's mouth. For example, when you say, "You don't know what you're talking about," you are sending a "you" message. An "I" message would be, "I get confused when you talk about several problems at one time. I don't understand what you're trying to say."

The "you" message lays blame on the speaker. The "I" message clarifies your concerns. It can be used effectively with a subordinate. An "I" message would be "When you aren't at work on time, I worry that you've been in an accident" or "When you come in late, I feel like you are purposely defying me." The "I" message tells the other person how you feel about a situation. The "I" message is concerned with the issue. The "you" message attacks the other person.

Practice "I" Messages

Directions: Rewrite the following "you" messages as "I" messages.

1.   "You're always late."
      Sample "I" message: *"When you are late, I feel like you are taking advantage of the company."*

      Your "I" Message:

2.   "You're never doing what you're supposed to be doing."
      Your "I" Message:

3.   "You should call me first."
      Your "I" Message:

4.   "You did it again. You screwed up the order."
      Your "I" Message:

> ## Technique # 5:
> ## Engage your brain and suspend your emotions.

"The mind of the intelligent seeks knowledge, but the mouth of the fool feeds on folly."

Proverbs 15:14

This is perhaps the hardest of the five techniques because verbal conflicts are emotional by nature. The ultimate goal is to turn the verbal conflict into a discussion. Verbal conflicts are counterproductive in conducting business, and they certainly don't foster a harmonious home life. Instead of letting your emotions take over, engage your brain and ask yourself, "What skills do I have that can help solve this problem? What solution is best for both of us? What is the problem and what can we change? What additional information do we need to analyze this problem?" You may have emotions, but you need to control them for the sake of the issue. Actively listen in a nonjudgmental way.

Example:

Your co-worker, May, stops by your workstation and says, "I don't understand why you're stabbing me in the back. You're going to get me fired if you don't stop it." This is obviously a potential verbal conflict charged with emotion. If you can control your emotions, you may say something like, "I hear you saying you're angry with me. Can you tell me how I've been stabbing you in the back?" You have responded objectively, intellectually and not emotionally.

> *"Emotion has taught mankind to reason."*
>
> *Marquis de Vauvenargues*

152

Other Techniques to Avoid Verbal Conflicts

Here are some other techniques you can use to avoid verbal conflicts.

- If at all possible, use a neutral territory when you think there may be a conflict. People are less likely to argue in public. Moving a business meeting to a more public place rather than a private office may force people to improve their behavior.

Neutral Territories

Directions: **List five neutral territories you could use to defuse a potentially volatile discussion.**

1. *I could schedule the contract meeting at a restaurant for a business luncheon.*

2.

3.

4.

5.

- Remember, it takes two to argue. The quickest way to defuse an argument is not to enter into it! For example, a co-worker says, "Todd's at it again. It's obvious that he's moving in on my territory. He's trying to take over. What are you going to do about it?" You know that the co-worker's problem is with Todd and that you don't want to be drawn into it. The co-worker is just looking for someone to bring into his fight with Todd. An appropriate response would be, "That's not my problem. You'll need to talk to Todd.".

How I Could Have Avoided Arguments by Not Entering into Them

Directions: List what you could have said to avoid any arguments you have been involved in recently.

---

1. *"I don't want to discuss this right now."*

2.

3.

4.

5.

- Find a place where you can actively listen to what the other person is saying. Avoid distractions. It is very hard to actively listen if you are being interrupted by the telephone, your secretary, your kids or the television.

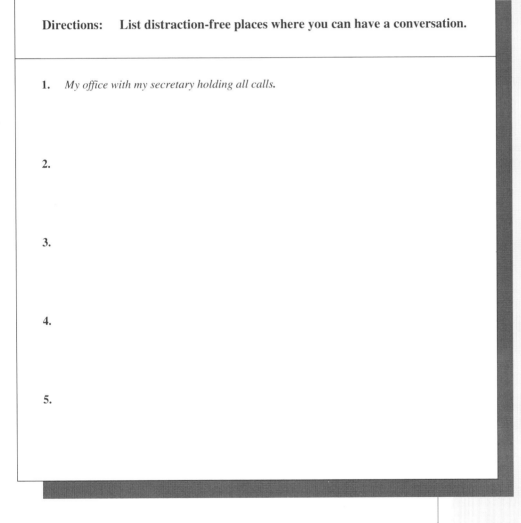

Places Without Distractions

Directions: List distraction-free places where you can have a conversation.

1. *My office with my secretary holding all calls.*

2.

3.

4.

5.

- Control the situation. Just because someone wants to discuss a problem right now does not mean that you have to stop what you are doing and enter the fray. If you feel that the moment is inappropriate or that you've been blind-sided and need time to prepare, schedule the "discussion" for a later time. This is obviously easier if you are in command. If you can't control the time, try to control where you sit, how prepared you are and how you look.

Discussions I Could Have Controlled

Directions: **List any recent discussions you had in which it would have been to your advantage to control the situation.**

1. *I wasn't prepared for my discussion about a raise with my boss.*

2.

3.

4.

5.

- Argue with your left brain. The left brain controls language and logic. Enter each discussion prepared to logically discuss the issues. The right brain controls your emotions and how you communicate nonverbally. Standing closer to a person, raising your voice and pointing your finger at someone in anger are all controlled by the right brain. Since up to 90 percent of what we communicate is nonverbal, be aware of your body language and its effect on others.

- Remember, you cannot change the past. You can only use it as a reference, not as a way of placing blame. Placing blame on another person may make you feel good, but it won't change the past. You can, however, control the future. Channel your energies into what is required to remedy the problem. Learn to reframe the argument — turn the conflict into resolution.

Example:

You have a running argument with your boss about how to schedule people who work for you. Until now you have blamed your boss for your workers' unhappiness with the schedule. In the past, he has insisted that they work late on Friday night so that they don't have to come in on Saturday morning to work. To reframe the argument you need to be able to see your boss's point of view and turn a current negative situation into a positive future situation. Instead of arguing on a right or wrong basis or blaming him for the problem, it makes more sense to work with your boss to find a resolution to the problem. Channel your energies positively instead of negatively.

> *"To make headway, improve your head."*
>
> *B.C. Forbes*

157

Reframing the Argument

Directions: Choose an argument you have recently had. Reframe the argument by identifying whom you blamed. What was the issue and what references were made to past problems? How could you have channeled your energies into resolving the issue?

Argument: *Argument with boss over scheduling*

Issue: *Whether my workers should work late on Friday night*

Person Blamed: *My boss*

References to Past Problems: *I've blamed him because of problems in scheduling holidays last year.*

How I Could Have Channeled My Energies to Resolve the Problem: *I should have gone to him with alternatives to scheduling.*

- Try for a win-win situation. In making decisions, a consensus is preferred because it leads to a solution. Each person has compromised somewhat, but everyone wins. In the previous example on scheduling work, one solution would be to meet with those scheduled to work. In participatory management, where workers have input, parameters would be outlined that the company could live with, such as finishing a certain amount of work by a certain time. Then, those who do the work would set their own schedules, making everyone happy while getting the work done.

Summary

You may not be able to avoid arguments and conflicts, but you can minimize their impact. By using the techniques described in this chapter and by better understanding the nature of verbal conflicts, you can control the number of conflicts you are involved in and develop skills that will help you find solutions. This does not mean that you will agree with everyone. You won't! But it does mean that you will defuse conflicts that tear relationships apart and get in the way of effective communication.

Review Questions:

1. What are the four characteristics of verbal conflicts?

2. In the past how have your listening skills contributed to verbal conflicts?

3. Which techniques can you put into practice immediately to minimize verbal conflicts?

4. Which techniques are you most likely to utilize?

CHAPTER 9

Understanding How You Communicate

While listening is extremely important, understanding how you communicate is equally important. Communication is a combination of speaking and listening. As an employee, you have certain ways of communicating that are more effective for you than others. However, you may be restricted in your means of communication by company policy or by your manager's style. For example, you may have to put all requests in writing because of company policy, yet your most effective form of communication may be one-to-one conversation.

> *"Can we talk?"*
>
> *Joan Rivers*

Communication Types Checklist

Directions: Listed below are the various types of communication found within a business setting. Check those you find most effective when communicating to your manager. For a review of the types of communication, see Chapter 8.

❏   Open communication network

❏   Chain communication network

❏   Central operator communication network

❏   Small group meetings

❏   Large group meetings

❏   Memos

❏   Newsletters

❏   Informal notes

❏   Informal one-to-one verbal communication

❏   Telephone one-to-one communication

❏   Telephone conferencing

❏   Formal group presentations

❏   Brainstorming situations

Communication Questions

1. **Are you restricted by company policy or managerial style in using some of these forms of communication?**

2. **What would happen if you used a different form than you normally do?**

3. **Why don't you use certain forms with your manager?**

Recognize Your Personal Communication Pitfalls

Communicating with and listening to your manager is different from communicating with and listening to those you manage. Your manager or supervisor has the power to evaluate you. Since his evaluation can affect your career and could even cost you your job, that evaluation should be the underlying premise in all your communication with management. It is important, therefore, that you recognize your personal communication patterns, mindsets and filters. That way you can control how you respond.

Key Idea:

> If you do not understand your personal communication patterns, you cannot actively listen, which could hamper your effectiveness as an employee. In the worst-case scenario, it

could result in your being fired. For example, if you do not realize that you are not effectively hearing your boss or your co-workers because of a cultural-background filter, you could end up with a poor evaluation and eventually lose your job.

Recognizing Your Personal Communication Patterns

Personal background can make a difference in the words and body language used for communication and listening. Following are a few of the differences that may affect your ability to listen: your order of birth in a family, your culture, the region you grew up in, your socioeconomic background, your family style, your religion, and the political makeup of your family. Each of these influences can impede or enhance effective communication.

Birth Order

The Oldest or Only Child:

Even a child with siblings is considered an only child if there are five years or more between him and a brother or sister. Like an only child, the oldest tends to be the one you can rely on. He is a perfectionist. Because parents usually have high expectations for their oldest, he tends to be serious and scholarly. He has to carry the banner for the family. Usually an overachiever, he sometimes becomes an underachiever because he cannot live up to his own or the family's ideals.

If you are an only or oldest child, you may be a perfectionist and will probably expect precise communication. You are used to being in charge and are more likely to give "commands." This may tend to make you a better talker than listener, or you will want to hear only what fits your expectations. You also will be more serious in your communication. Be aware that a person who jokes also can be serious. Remember that decisions can be made without everything being perfect. As an only or first child, you need to work hard to practice Active and Reflective Listening.

My Action Plan to Improve My Listening Skills as a First or Only Child

My Action Plan:

Goals to Accomplish:

Obstacles Keeping Me from Accomplishing These Goals:

Steps to Accomplish These Goals:

Time Line for Accomplishing These Goals:

Keep these same communication tendencies in mind when you work with individuals who are only or first children.

Oldest or Only Children in My Workplace

1.

2.

3.

4.

5.

The Middle Child:

The middle child must find a niche for himself, so he takes on characteristics that are opposite of those of the first child. If you are a middle child, you tend to be the mediator in the family or the peacemaker, a role that carries over into the workplace. You don't like conflict. While the oldest child looks for guidance from his parents, the middle child has extreme loyalty to his peers. He is seen by many as a maverick and an independent. As a middle child, be aware that you are used to compromise, although you may not like it. You may secretly rebel against it. You may send reconciliatory messages to avoid conflict, only to be frustrated later. You are used to practicing Reflective Listening. You have a tendency to side with your peers instead of thinking for yourself. Unfortunately, this is not an effective way to make business decisions.

My Action Plan to Improve My Listening Skills as a Middle Child

My Action Plan:

Goals to Accomplish:

Obstacles Keeping Me from Accomplishing These Goals:

Steps to Accomplish These Goals:

Time Line for Accomplishing These Goals:

Keep these same communication tendencies in mind when you work with individuals who are middle children.

Middle Children in My Workplace

1.

2.

3.

4.

5.

The Youngest Child:

The youngest child is a people person. As the youngest, you, too, have had to carve out your niche in the family. You are usually charming, a "sales" person, but you are also manipulative, having learned the "ways of the world" from your older siblings. Since you are the "baby" of the family, you are often treated as a baby, a term you generally hate. You learn that showing off and blaming others is tolerated because you are the youngest.

Your learned behavior of being the "baby" is carried over into adulthood. You are likely to hear only what you want to hear. Your tendency to manipulate affects your ability to listen and communicate. As a speaker, remember that you may frustrate the receiver with "immature" or manipulative behavior. If you are the listener, you may have to fight your tendency to hear only what pleases you. However, you will probably relate well to your audience.

My Action Plan to Improve My Listening Skills as the Youngest Child

My Action Plan:

Goals to Accomplish:

Obstacles Keeping Me from Accomplishing These Goals:

Steps to Accomplish These Goals:

Time Line for Accomplishing These Goals:

Keep the same communication tendencies in mind when you work with individuals who are youngest children.

Youngest Children in My Workplace

1.

2.

3.

4.

5.

This is a rather simplistic treatment of birth order. Larger families and stepfamilies further complicate the basic issue. Although this is not a complete explanation, it illustrates how a person's position in the family may affect his communication and listening.

Cultural Background

Our culture is made up of the ideas, rituals and ethnicity we grow up with. Since we are a nation of immigrants, varying degrees of immigrant cultures affect us, including the prevailing American culture, and several subcultures. This melting pot can affect how we communicate and listen.

Example:

If a listener comes from a predominantly German-American culture and the speaker comes from a predominantly Chinese-American culture, they may filter the communication through their differing cultural backgrounds. For example, if they are discussing whether there should be a beer tent at the annual company picnic, their cultures may affect their discussion. A beer tent would be quite acceptable in the German-American culture, but considered strange in the Chinese-American culture.

Cultural Background Check

Directions: Identify the cultural background for each of the following:

1. **My cultural background:**

2. **My manager's cultural background:**

3. **My co-workers' cultural backgrounds:**

4. **My employees' cultural backgrounds:**

How do these backgrounds affect communication and listening?

The American culture puts a great emphasis on self-reliance coupled with an open and friendly attitude. If your firm is located in a community where a subculture emphasizes working together as a team in a formal manner, you may find communication difficult or slow. You will need to adjust your method of communication and practice Active Listening to gain an understanding of that subculture.

Understanding another's cultural background may take time. An open mind and Active Listening can help you achieve this understanding.

- Be aware of the various cultures or subcultures of your co-workers, your boss and those you manage.

- Understanding a culture different from your own does not mean that you have to embrace it or adopt it. However, such an understanding will promote better listening and communication. Reflective Listening also will help.

- Take time to discuss some of the differences you are aware of with those who are of a different culture. Do not be judgmental. That will only erect communication barriers.

"The great law of culture is: Let each become all that he was created capable of being."

Thomas Carlyle

Cultural Differences That Affect Communication in My Workplace

Directions: List those people whom you work with. Then identify the cultural differences that you have noticed and indicate how they affect effective listening.

Name	Cultural Difference	Effect It Has on Listening
Madge	*Comes from Swedish-American background*	*Seems rather formal and aloof*

- Learn what the limits are. For example, if your employee's subculture demands more personal space in a conversation, learn how close you may come before violating his or her personal space.

Regional Background

If you have traveled to another part of the United States, you are aware of how regional backgrounds can affect communication. Regional backgrounds are similar to a person's culture, but refer specifically to the way things are done and said in a particular region of the country. For instance, a person's dialect and accent can affect how you listen. If you have grown up believing that a person who has a Southern accent is slow and not too smart, then you will have difficulty accepting your new boss from Mississippi when he speaks. Unfortunately, most of our filters that affect communication are based on stereotypes. The fact that your new boss has his M.B.A. from Harvard is overlooked when he opens his mouth. This problem in communication is further compounded if he uses regional expressions that you don't understand. Although television has done much to erase some of the regional differences in language, they still exist.

- Take time to learn what the regional expressions or words mean. Today's mobility in business means that you will come in contact with people from backgrounds different from your own.

Regional Terms That Have Affected My Listening at Work

Directions: **List any regional terms that have gotten in the way of your listening to another worker. Give a definition of that term.**

Term	Meaning
Davenport	*A sofa or couch; term used in parts of the Midwest*

- Be aware of your own regional dialect or expressions.
  Don't be so provincial that you believe that everyone has
  an accent or a dialect but you.

My Regional Expressions That May Impede Communication

Directions: List your regional expressions that may get in the way of
someone understanding you.

Expression	What It Means
Plum tuckered out	*Very tired*

- If you don't understand what is said, ask the sender to repeat or to clarify.

- Keep an open mind when confronted with regional dialects or expressions. Maybe you've always called a meal where everyone brings a dish to share a "potluck." That doesn't mean that the term "carry-in dinner" is incorrect. It's just another way of saying the same thing.

Socioeconomic Background

Liza Doolittle in *My Fair Lady* is a good example of how different socioeconomic backgrounds can affect communication. Henry Higgins' quest to change Liza into a high-society lady is the basis for this delightful musical filled with communication problems. Luckily, Americans are a bit more mobile. Our dialects and accents aren't based on socioeconomics to the extent that English society was at the time of *My Fair Lady*. However, socioeconomic backgrounds still affect communication today, both in speaking and listening.

For example, an older worker who grew up during the Depression may filter economic information. He might have trouble hearing that it is good to spend money instead of saving it in some instances. His socioeconomic upbringing has taught him to be frugal and wary of spending too much.

An awareness of your co-workers' socioeconomic backgrounds, both past and present, can help you build solid relationships. Having a company picnic catered may seem like a good idea. However, if your co-workers' socioeconomic backgrounds make them view this as a frivolous expense, it might be better to cancel the picnic and use the money in an incentive program.

- Take time to know the socioeconomic backgrounds of those you communicate with and adjust your conversations accordingly.

- Listen carefully and question the speaker if you don't understand. For example, if you are debating an issue and the speaker keeps using polo terminology to make his point, swallow your pride and ask him to explain the analogy. A good communicator always considers the knowledge and experience of his listeners.

- Just because someone belongs to the same socioeconomic group that you do, don't assume that he always has. America prides itself on the opportunity for anyone to move up the socioeconomic scale. He may look the part, but in his heart and mind he may carry many of the socioeconomic filters from his past. The converse may be true also. He may filter everything from his new station in life, meaning that he won't consider any idea that smacks of his past. For example, if your manager comes from a poor family of nine, and has made a success of himself, he may filter out anything that reminds him of his past.

"Human status ought not to depend upon the changing demands of the economic process."

William Temple

Family Style

David Field, in his book *Family Personalities,* identifies five different family personalities: bonding, ruling, protecting, chaotic and symbiotic. The bonding family is ideal. It strikes a balance between being an individual and being part of a close-knit relationship. The ruling family is controlled by authoritarian parents, so children often feel uncared for. The protecting family is characterized by parents who do too much for their children. The chaotic family acts more like roommates than a family. They are just people living under the same roof. The symbiotic family works only as a group; individuality is forbidden. Each of these family styles affects the relationships found within the families.

Another way of looking at family style is found in my book, *Parenting: Ward and June Don't Live Here Anymore.* * Here, I break families into six different parenting styles: dictator, benevolent dictator, president's council, family council, egalitarian and manipulative. The dictator family is run by one autocratic parent. What he says is the law. The benevolent-dictator style is similar. Although it is run by one parent, the parent appears to be kind until someone steps out of line. The president's council is governed by one or both parents, who have ultimate veto power. The rest of the family operates on an advise-and-consent basis. The family council, on the other hand, empowers each member of the family to have a say in what happens in the family. The egalitarian family stresses the individuality of each member, and as long as they don't step on each other's toes, the family can function. In the manipulative family, each member manipulates the others to get his own way. As you can see, the makeup and style of one's family affect communication and listening.

* This book is available through National Press Publications, 1-800-258-7246.

If you have grown up in a family that yells and argues — everyone talking at once and gesturing wildly with their hands — you will feel most comfortable with that manner of communication. You know the rules and how they work. Therefore, you may find it very frustrating to calmly present your ideas and listen to everyone else's presentation. If, on the other hand, you have grown up in a family that communicates through manipulation of emotions, you may find it difficult to communicate and listen logically. You likely will rely on body language and carefully chosen words to manipulate your listener's emotions. To overcome these family influences, follow these guidelines.

- Be aware of your own family's communication process and how it affects you.

Family-Communication Awareness Check

1. **Which family personality or parenting style did you grow up with?**

2. **How did your family communicate?**

3. **Who had the power?**

4. **Did family members communicate through logic, emotion, status of the speaker, body language or sheer volume?**

- Identify the filters from your family background that affect your listening. For example, if your parents always stressed how important it was to have money, you will tend to filter what is said to you accordingly. So if a co-worker talks about his decision not to pursue a career advancement because he'd rather be happy than rich, you may have trouble listening effectively to him.

Family-Filter Awareness Check

1. Were there certain forbidden topics in your family that you still have trouble listening to? List them.

2. Were there certain phrases that triggered a negative or positive response among family members? List them.

3. Were there certain gestures that were not allowed in your family or were there gestures that were encouraged? List them.

4. How does your family background affect your listening?

5. What can you do to change this?

- Discuss family communication styles with your co-workers and with your family members to identify ways to improve your communication with them.

My Co-Workers' Family Communication Styles

Directions: **List below the names of your co-workers and their family style of communication. Then indicate how you can improve your communication with them.**

Person	Style	Ways to Improve Communication

Religious Background

For some, religious upbringing provides a powerful communication filter, but for others it has little effect. Check your own religious filters in the following exercise.

Religious-Filter Check

Directions: How does your religious background affect your listening skills? Respond by writing your reaction to each of the following words or phrases. Analyze how your reaction affects your ability to listen to someone who uses these words.

Abortions

Pro-choice

Pro-life

Euthanasia

AIDS

Homosexual ministers

Welfare

Environmentally safe

Sex education

You probably work with people of many religious backgrounds. You may even fall in love and marry someone of a different religion. Since religion is an emotionally charged topic, some communication can be touchy between people of different religious backgrounds. Luckily, we live in a country founded on religious freedom, so we have learned to be somewhat tolerant of other people's religions. Keep these guidelines in mind to become even more tolerant.

- Find out what your co-workers' religious backgrounds are and how their religions view life. For example, knowing that three out of five of your immediate co-workers' religions stress community involvement in social issues can help you better understand their reluctance to working overtime because they are heavily committed outside of the workday.

Co-Workers' Religious Backgrounds

Directions: List the names and religions of your co-workers. Then indicate how their religious backgrounds affect their communication.

Name	Religion	How the Religion Affects Their Communication
Ryan	*Episcopal*	*Tends to be liberal and willing to listen*

- Be aware of religion-associated words that may trigger emotional responses in both you and your co-workers. Words such as "born-again," "abortion" and "evangelical" are examples. Try to avoid such words, if possible.

Religious Words Worksheet

Directions: **List religion-associated words that may trigger emotional responses in you and your co-workers and affect listening.**

Example: *crucifix, home schooling, fundamentalist*

- If necessary, avoid certain topics if you and the person you are communicating with cannot agree to disagree. If you and a co-worker do not see eye to eye on women in the ministry, for example, agree to disagree rather than argue.

- Respect your co-worker's right to bow out of a conversation or to change the subject if he is uncomfortable with it because of his religion. If during lunch, the topic of sex education in the schools comes up, some co-workers may choose to leave or you may want to change the subject.

- Be aware of your co-workers' religious customs, including holidays. This is especially important during December, when both Christmas and Hanukkah are celebrated.

Political Background

Just as with religion, some people grew up in stronger politically oriented homes than others. Political, in the broadest sense of the word, refers to whether you see life conservatively, liberally or somewhere in between. Everyone has a political viewpoint, and each political viewpoint comes with its own set of filters that affect communication. If you know your boss is conservative and you are liberal, listening to a radically new idea for the company will result in two very different responses. Both of you will run the idea through your respective political filters and approve or disapprove it, rationalizing.

Example:

Let's say that the international sales manager in your company wants to make a trade agreement with a company in a third-world nation that supports South Africa. Your boss, because of his political background, says that it's necessary only to look at the other company's record and the potential for profit for your company. You, on the other hand, feel strongly that there should be a sanction on trade with South Africa and any company doing business with yours should have the same policy. Both of you are listening to the presentation by the international sales manager through your political filters. Political and religious-background filters are perhaps the touchiest in communication. To help overcome them, practice these steps.

- Be aware of the political background of co-workers. This will help you avoid sensitive subjects and understand the filters at work when you and they communicate.

> *"Man is by nature a political animal."*
>
> *Aristotle*

- Realize that you cannot change a person's political background and that every conversation does not need to cause political sparring.

- Decide which issues are important to fight for and which are not. For example, even though you may feel strongly about labor unions, you need to decide if that is an issue that is important enough to fight for and consequently put your reputation and perhaps even your job on the line.

- Listen carefully to what the other person is saying, even though you may not agree with him politically.

- Be aware of your own political "red flags" when listening. Do you see red when someone mentions capital-gains taxes or free marketing? These are words that may cause you to hear only your side.

My Personal Political "Red Flags" That Affect My Listening

Directions: List those words, phrases or topics that are your political red flags.

Words/Phrases/Topics	**Emotion**
Trickle-down economics	*Instantly defensive*

- Practice Active Listening

Although you may not be able to know everything about everyone you speak to and listen to, it is helpful to know as much as you can about the person you're communicating with. A person's background, both open and hidden, definitely affects his ability to communicate and to listen effectively.

Summary

Knowing how you and others communicate will help you be a better listener. Our emotional and mental filters are affected by our backgrounds. If you can assess your own filters and assess those of other people, you are on your way to being an effective listener.

Review Questions:

1. How does your birth order affect your communication with your co-workers?

2. How do your co-workers' birth orders affect their communication?

3. In what ways does a person's religious background affect his communication?

4. How does your family-style background affect your ability to listen?

5. After doing the exercises in this chapter, what were you most surprised to learn about your own or your fellow workers' communication?

*C*HAPTER 10

Listening to People You Work with

At work, much of your day is spent in listening situations. This chapter will show you how to apply Active and Reflective Listening techniques to some of the more common listening situations you may encounter.

A Memory Device for Active Listening

Remember the following simple memory device to use when practicing Active Listening. Each letter in the word **LLAMA** stands for one of the steps to follow in Active Listening.

L	=	**Listen to the content.**
L	=	**Listen to the intent.**
A	=	**Assess the speaker's nonverbal communication and background.**
M	=	**Monitor your nonverbal communication and background.**
A	=	**Answer the co-worker with empathy and without judgment.**

L
L
A
M
A

L
L
A
M
A

Listen to the content.   [L] L A M A

Much of what is communicated on a daily basis is content—the nuts and bolts of a business operation. These details are essential. If you don't understand, ask for a clarification.

Listen to the intent.   L [L] A M A

Listen to the emotional meaning. Is the speaker communicating through the role he is playing? Is he filtering out certain information because of his personal filters? Listening to the intent becomes particularly important in decision-making situations.

Assess the speaker's nonverbal communication and background.   L L [A] M A

Read and interpret what the speaker is "saying" with his nonverbal communication. Interpret what the speaker is "saying" by understanding his background and personality. Once again, this understanding will result in you being better able to respond to the real reason why someone says what he says.

Monitor your nonverbal communication and background.
L L A [M] A

Be aware of the message you are sending with your nonverbal communication. Be aware of your own emotional filters that affect your understanding of the sender.

Answer the co-worker with empathy and without judgment.
L L A M [A]

If you take all of the other aspects of **LLAMA** into consideration, the last will come fairly easily. Answering the speaker with empathy sends the signal that you understand him and that you will take his feelings into consideration when you respond. Answering the speaker in a nonjudgmental way sends the signal that he and his communication are worthwhile. It also sends the signal that you respect what he has to say.

Put LLAMA into Effect.

Listening to Your Manager

To be a good employee, you must also be a good listener. For example, if you do not listen carefully, you may miss deadlines or misinterpret company policy. To effectively communicate with and listen to your superiors, you need to follow these techniques.

Techniques to Effectively Listen to Your Managers:

- Recognize the filters that affect your ability to listen. Are there certain ideas that you automatically prejudge? For example, do you filter everything through your "Union Filter" or through your "I'm-Due-for-a-Raise Filter"? If so, learn to control them.

- Know those who manage you. Knowing your manager's emotional and mental filters will help you interpret what he is saying. It also will allow you to respond in a manner that ensures you will be heard. For example, your manager loves to talk about cars, so you compare your performance with a car. His emotional filter will cue in on the car and help him remember what you were talking about.

- Active Listening can help you. If you don't listen actively, you may miss part of your boss's message that will ultimately make the difference in your job. If your boss says that a particular report must be on his desk in one week and you miss the deadline because you weren't listening, your job may be affected.

There are five steps that can help you communicate better with your boss.

Five Steps to Effective Communication with Your Boss

1. Recognize your personal style of following.

2. Identify your most effective means of communication and listening.

3. Recognize your personal communication/listening pitfalls.

4. Know those who manage you.

5. Put Active Listening into effect.

Recognize Your Personal Style of Following

Every employee has his own personal style of following or being supervised. However, the role you play may vary from time to time and from situation to situation. Following are a few of the roles employees play when being managed. Try to identify which role you mostly play in your business. Do any of these fit you?

Types of Roles Employees Play

The Mediator

Like the peacemaker in a group disagreement, the mediator sees his role as keeping everybody happy. He spends much time among his peers patching up relations and even resolving conflicts between his manager and other employees. He is invaluable when communication is poor because he is a very Active Listener. He uses Reflective Listening effectively, and most co-workers trust him. However, he is also likely to suffer from burnout because of the burden he has taken on.

The Brown-Noser

This person always looks good in front of his superiors. He agrees with everything they say and dutifully carries out their orders. Generally, he is disliked by his peers and is quite often used by his managers. He practices Selective Listening by listening to only those things that will make him look good. Despite his desire to please, he is not seen as a leader and is in a dead-end position. Even more sadly, he doesn't realize the role he is playing and how it affects his career.

The Company Man

Often mistaken as a Brown-Noser, the Company Man wholeheartedly believes the company credo and all it stands for. He is here to stay. He is different from the Brown-Noser because he does not say yes to everything. He has his goals and aspirations and is probably pragmatic. He will do whatever it takes to keep his career on track with the company. He practices Active Listening because his career is at stake.

The Rebel

There are actually three different types of rebels within a company: the Sanctioned Rebel, the Active Rebel and the Quiet Rebel.

The Sanctioned Rebel

The Sanctioned Rebel has official standing, such as being a union steward. The company recognizes his right to disagree because he officially represents opposition to the management. Managers expect him to be in disagreement. Usually, the Sanctioned Rebel is an Active Listener because of the role he plays. However, because of his "rebel" filters he can easily become a Selective Listener. For example, when management starts talking about layoffs, his "rebel" filters kick in. If he is actively listening, he will hear what management is saying and then make a decision based on serving the union's best interests. If he is selectively listening, his decision will be based only on what he wants to hear and may work against those he represents.

The Active Rebel

The Active Rebel is a role that some employees take on because they want to change the company; others assume it because they are fed up with management. The Active Rebel usually doesn't stay with the company very long because he is either fired or quits. The Active Rebel tends to be a very selective listener.

The Quiet Rebel

The Quiet Rebel often appears to be doing his work, but is in fact rebelling by doing only those things he sees as important. In some cases, he is quietly undermining management. He disagrees with management, but not enough to lose his job. He, too, hears only what he wants to hear.

The Leave Me Alone

This role is played for a number of reasons, but in all cases the employee just wants to be left alone. He doesn't want to become involved in decisions, changes, office politics and, in the extreme, the social life of the business. Sometimes this role is taken on because the employee has gotten burnt or been disappointed once too often, and other times it is because the employee is suffering from burnout. Employees near retirement often play this game. The Leave Me Alone filters out anything that would cause him to become actively involved in the company.

The Ambitious — Positive

This is the person who wants a promotion and goes about it in a positive way. He is actively seeking advancement. Many times he plays the role of Company Man at the same time. He practices Active Listening.

The Ambitious — Negative

This is the person who wants a promotion and will go to any means to get it, including backstabbing. This person subscribes to the maxim, "You don't have to worry about hurting those on your way up if you don't plan on coming back down again." He is usually power hungry and often brown-noses when it is convenient to do so. He practices Selective Listening.

The Hard Worker

Of course, we would all like to think we play this role. The Hard Worker does his job, stays on tasks, meets deadlines and is respected by his peers. He is not actively seeking advancement, but accepts it as it comes along. His listening tends to be selective, hearing only what has to be done. However, he also may practice Active and Reflective Listening.

"There is no substitute for hard work."

Thomas Edison

Roles Played at Work

Directions: Identify those people you work with who fit into the roles just described.

Mediators

1.

2.

3.

Quiet Rebels

1.

2.

3.

Brown-Nosers

1.

2.

3.

Leave Me Alones

1.

2.

3.

Company Men

1.

2.

3.

Ambitious — Positives

1.

2.

3.

Sanctioned Rebels

1.

2.

3.

Ambitious — Negatives

1.

2.

3.

Active Rebels

1.

2.

3.

Hard Workers

1.

2.

3.

Questions

1. How does the role affect their ability to listen?

2. If they became better listeners, would the role change?

3. What can I learn from their listening skills, or which of their listening skills should I avoid?

These are only a few of the roles found within a group of employees. Which do you identify with? Who in your office, department or company plays these roles? You or they may even play a combination of roles.

My Role at Work

The role I play in my business is _____

_____

_____.

The reason I play this role is that _____

_____

_____.

The type of listening that I use in this role is _____

_____

_____.

How Active and Reflective Listening would affect the role I play:

Case Study:

Upon arriving back from lunch, you hear the following
conversation about possible layoffs in the plant:

Cathy: Personally, I don't think I'll be hit. I'm good friends
with the boss. Our families go way back.

Joe: Well, the union certainly doesn't like it. Since I'm in charge of negotiations, you can be sure that we'll do everything to stop the layoffs.

George: Typical management. They screwed us out of our pension, now they're screwing us out of our jobs.

Milly: Well, the way I look at it, they have no choice. Considering the recession, what can they do? If the company's to survive, they have to cut workers. What do you think, Frank?

Frank: Me? I'd rather not get involved.

Sidney: Sure, put your head in the sand, Frank.

Ruth: Sidney, let Frank be. You know he's just thinking about retirement.

Case Study Questions:

1. Which employee is playing the role of Sanctioned Rebel?

2. Which is playing the role of Brown-Noser?

3. Which is playing the role of Mediator?

4. Which is playing the role of Leave Me Alone?

5. Which is playing the role of Company Man?

6. Which is playing the role of Active Rebel?

C A S E   S T U D Y

Listening to Your Co-Workers

Although more and more businesses are using a "teamwork" approach to management, competition among co-workers still exists. When you compete with those you work with, Active Listening can give you the edge. If you are lucky enough to be in a teamwork situation, Active Listening will make you a better team member.

Communicating with your co-workers and listening to them actively is usually easier than communicating with and listening to your managers or those you manage. Your co-workers are the people you work with every day, and you should know them fairly well. In many cases, they are among the people you socialize with. As friends, you probably communicate very well. However, there are also people in your immediate department or team that you don't know very well. These are the people you are most likely to have problems communicating with. Since you have to work together, particularly if your company emphasizes a team concept, you will want to maximize your communication through Active Listening.

Active Listening Techniques to Make You More Competitive:

- Active Listening allows you to hear the whole message. If you hear only part of the message, you may make poor decisions or fail to fully complete a task. For example, if because of poor listening you hear only that a report on employee benefits needs to be done, but not when it needs to be done, you may not be able to complete the task.

- Active Listening allows you to read a person's nonverbal communication and tailor your response to it. If your manager is frowning when you mention taking time off, you may want to bring the topic up later or talk to him about it in a way that is more acceptable.

- Active Listening makes you look good because you always seem on top of things. You respond to the total communication.

Active Listening Techniques to Help You Be a Better Team Member:

- In a competitive work situation, Active Listening allows you to hear the whole message, verbal and nonverbal. If you hear only part of the message, you can't do your best job. If your manager gives you instructions and you carry out only half of them because you were not actively listening, you will not keep your competitive edge.

"You're either part of the solution or part of the problem."

Eldridge Cleaver

- Active Listening helps you keep the team focused if others are distracted and not actively listening. As an Active Listener, you can direct your comments and questions so that the team gets back on track.

- Active Listening promotes cooperation by making you view situations in an empathic and nonjudgmental way.

Steps I Can Take to Become a More Active Listener in a Team Situation

Directions: List those steps that you can take to improve your listening in a team situation.

1. *I will try to be aware of the nonverbal communication used by my team.*

2.

3.

4.

5.

There Are Five Ways to Improve Communication with Your Co-Workers

1. Recognize your personal role in communicating with your co-workers.

2. Identify your most effective means of communication.

3. Recognize your personal communication and listening pitfalls.

4. Know your co-workers.

5. Put LLAMA into effect.

Technique #1:
Recognize Your Personal Role in Communicating with Your Co-Workers

Although no official script is directing co-workers, roles are played nonetheless. The following descriptions may help you identify the role you play. Incidentally, the role may be the same as the one you play as an employee, or it may be different. Some of the styles of communication used by people playing these roles are formal, while others are informal.

Role 1: The Mediator

The Mediator is likely to play this role both as co-worker and as employee. He spends a great amount of time patching up disagreements and mediating among department or team members. He uses a central operator communication network, making himself the central operator. He is the one everybody goes to with their problems. Naturally, he is a good listener, particularly a Reflective Listener.

Role 2: The Rebel

As in the employee-management relationship, co-workers play different types of Rebels: the Sanctioned Rebel and the Active Rebel.

A: The Sanctioned Rebel

Within a group of co-workers, the Sanctioned Rebel plays an important role because he communicates concerns and disagreements with management. He brings a message to management and then takes its response back. To do so, he uses a chain network. His function is to help co-workers communicate to management about rules, regulations and work conditions. He practices Active Listening; however, he can easily end up using Selective Listening.

B: The Active Rebel

The Active Rebel among co-workers can be a threat. Because he is not sanctioned by management, he is always asking his co-workers to put their jobs on the line for something he is rebelling against. He listens selectively, filtering everything he disagrees with.

Role 3: The "Greta Garbo" — "I 'Vant' to Be Alone"

If you play this role in your department or team, you prefer not to communicate with your co-workers or to keep communication to a minimum. You just want to do your job and be left alone. Your choice of isolation may be caused by a variety of reasons—everything from feeling that you are not a part of the group to basically disliking the group members. If you listen at all, you listen only selectively.

Role 4: The Team Player

This person spends much of his time communicating with the other team members. He is an Active Listener and uses an open communication network. He is positive and wants the team to function well. He takes the time to communicate with and listen to the others on his team.

> *"I hold it, that a little rebellion, now and then, is a good thing."*
>
> *Thomas Jefferson*

201

Role 5: The Conservator

This person has taken on the role of making sure the department or team conserves its resources and time. He believes that change is good only if it takes the past into consideration. He also believes that you shouldn't fix something if it isn't broken. He listens selectively through his conservative filter.

Role 6: The "Let's Change It"

This role is the direct opposite of the Conservator. He is ready to make changes, and his personal communication filter sees change for the better. Like the Active Rebel, he often asks his co-workers to stick their necks out for his cause. He tends to listen selectively. Unless they are both trying their hardest to use Active Listening, the Conservator and the "Let's Change It" will clash.

Role 7: The Negative

In most cases, this person communicates negatively to his co-workers. For him, nothing is ever right in his life, the company's life or his co-workers' lives. Understanding this person can be frustrating, and it is difficult to respond to him in a nonjudgmental way. His negative attitude affects his listening ability—he hears either too little or too much, whatever it takes to validate his negativism.

Role 8: The Social Butterfly

Although this person may be a hard worker, his primary concern when it comes to communication is "let's have fun." He organizes company social functions and spends a great amount of time on nonbusiness discussions. He is usually an Active Listener but can get sidetracked if something social comes up.

Role 9: The Organizer

The Organizer is not only organized himself, he also organizes other people's lives, voluntarily and sometimes involuntarily. When needed, he usually organizes the department or team, such as by setting up meetings. But his organizing filter can get in the way, too. For example, he doesn't like activities like brainstorming because he views them as messy and unpredictable.

Role 10: The Encyclopedia

On the positive side, this co-worker can answer anything because he has all of the answers. On the negative side, he butts in and tells you how to do everything. He tends to filter for misinformation, making sure everything is correct. As a result, he often misses the point.

Roles Co-Workers Play

Directions: Identify the roles your co-workers play.

Mediators in My Workplace:
1.
2.
3.

"Let's-Change-Its" in My Workplace:
1.
2.
3.

Sanctioned Rebels in My Workplace:
1.
2.
3.

Negatives in My Workplace:
1.
2.
3.

Active Rebels in My Workplace:
1.
2.
3.

Social Butterflies in My Workplace:
1.
2.
3.

Greta Garbos in My Workplace:
1.
2.
3.

Organizers in My Workplace:
1.
2.
3.

Team Players in My Workplace:
1.
2.
3.

Encyclopedias in My Workplace:
1.
2.
3.

Conservators in My Workplace:
1.
2.
3.

Questions

1.   How do your co-workers' roles affect their ability to listen?

2   How do these roles affect your ability to listen to them?

3.   Which of your co-workers' listening techniques should you avoid?

Technique #2:
Identify Your Most Effective Means
of Communication

As an employee communicating with your manager, you may be
restricted in the type of communication you use. That is usually not
true among co-workers. The vast majority of communication within
a department or among team members is verbal. That is why Active
Listening is so important for co-workers.

Co-Worker Communication Checklist

Directions: Check the types of communication you have found most effective with your co-workers.

❑   Open communication network

❑   Chain communication network

❑   Central operator communication network

❑   Small group meetings

❑   Large group meetings

❑   Memos

❑   Newsletters

❑   Informal notes

❑   Informal one-to-one verbal communication

❑   Telephone one-to-one communication

❑   Telephone conferencing

❑   Formal group presentations

❑   Brainstorming situations

❑   Suggestion box

Are most of these verbal?

In which of the types checked could you use Active Listening?

Even if you use a written form of communication most often, you can still practice Active Listening. LLAMA works just as well for written as for spoken communication. Both rely on the content and the intent. Written language uses nonverbals, too, such as the form of the communication, the handwriting and the tone of the letter.

Technique #3:
Recognize Your Personal Communication and Listening Pitfalls

While your co-workers do not have the power to formally evaluate you or fire you, they can help make your life wonderful or miserable. These are the people you work with every day, and the more communication pitfalls you encounter, the harder it is to actively listen. Most likely, the biggest communication pitfall will come from "personality clashes." It's helpful for you to identify your communication blocks to different types of personalities. If someone makes you see red whenever he opens his mouth, try to identify what angers you. It may be that he reminds you of someone else, like your irresponsible younger brother.

"Know then thyself, presume not God to scan; the proper study of mankind is man."

Alexander Pope

Identifying Communication Blocks for Co-workers:

Directions: List the names of your co-workers. For each of the co-workers listed, answer the following questions.

Names of Co-Workers:

1. Are you angry because of their personalities?

2. Do they remind you of someone from your past whom you didn't get along with?

3. Do they upset you because of what they say or because of certain situations?

Playing amateur psychologist can help you understand why Active Listening is so difficult with certain people. If you can identify the problem, you can eliminate or at least neutralize it, and then work on Active Listening.

Technique #4:
Know Your Co-Workers

This should be easy because these are the people you work with on a daily basis. In fact, some of them may be your good friends. Since you do work with them closely and need to communicate and listen to them daily, it is important that you learn their personal communication tendencies. Even if you are not close friends, you still need a basic understanding of the communication blocks they may have. The longer you work with a person, the easier it should be for you to communicate with and actively listen to him. Understanding his personal communication patterns can help you tailor what you are "sending" to him. You cannot assume that he is always actively listening to you. So knowing what he will not hear will help you know what to say and how to say it.

When in doubt about communicating with somebody at work, keep these three simple rules in mind:

Know your audience.
Know yourself.
Adjust accordingly.

Technique #5:
Put LLAMA into Effect

Once you have dealt with the previous four techniques to improve communication with your co-workers, it is time to put LLAMA to work. Since much of the workday is spent listening, Active Listening is vitally important. By listening to the content and intent of your co-workers, assessing their nonverbal signals and background, monitoring your own nonverbal signals and background, and finally by responding to your co-workers with empathy and without judgment, you will improve communication at your place of work.

Listening to Those You Manage

Effective management requires Active Listening. If you do not listen to those you manage, you are headed for morale problems and inefficient work. Use both Active and Reflective Listening when managing. Usually, the more you listen, the better you manage.

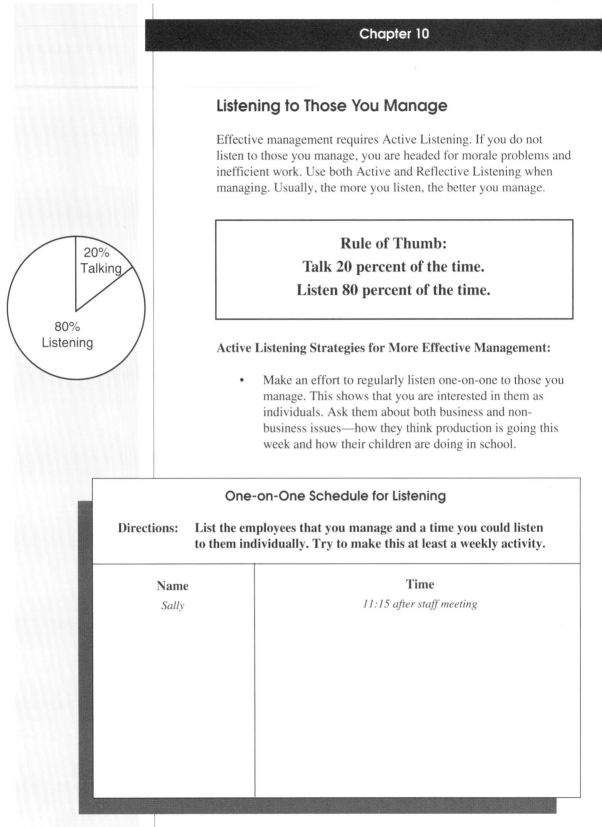

20% Talking

80% Listening

Rule of Thumb:

Talk 20 percent of the time.

Listen 80 percent of the time.

Active Listening Strategies for More Effective Management:

- Make an effort to regularly listen one-on-one to those you manage. This shows that you are interested in them as individuals. Ask them about both business and non-business issues—how they think production is going this week and how their children are doing in school.

One-on-One Schedule for Listening

Directions: List the employees that you manage and a time you could listen to them individually. Try to make this at least a weekly activity.

Name	Time
Sally	*11:15 after staff meeting*

- Use Reflective Listening to help those you manage solve their own problems. This makes you look good because you haven't dictated a solution. Also, it helps the employee "buy into" the solution and implementation. If an employee complains that he doesn't have enough time to eat, use Reflective Listening to help him find a solution.

- Know your employees' emotional and mental filters. Doing so will help you listen to what they are saying and also help you understand them. If you have an employee who has recently gone through a divorce and seems easily distracted, you will be better able to understand him because of your knowledge of his emotional filters.

- Remove barriers that impede listening when talking with your employees. Get out from behind your desk. Walk around your work area each day.

- Listening with empathy sends a powerful message that you care about your employees' ideas. Empathic listening is nonjudgmental, so it encourages communication between your employees and you. For example, if an employee had an idea that would streamline production and reduce injuries by 30 percent, you would probably have no trouble listening to him. If the next day, however, he had an idea that would increase production costs by 50 percent, you would be less likely to listen. If you practice empathic listening, your employee will get the message that the door is open to new ideas even though they may not be accepted.

- Listen without judging. By not immediately evaluating, you encourage new ideas and open communication lines. When an employee criticizes one of your policies, you might be tempted to "turn him off." However, if you listen in a nonjudgmental way to what he says, he will realize there is open communication. You may find a way to change a policy so that it works better for everyone.

- Regularly schedule brainstorming sessions for problem-solving. Then, sit back and listen.

Listening in Meetings

Listening in meetings can be frustrating because you often are thinking about what you are going to say while someone is still speaking. If you don't, someone else will start talking and you may miss your chance. At the same time, it can be frustrating when others are not listening, get off the topic or repeat what's already been said.

Use These Techniques to Effectively Listen in Meetings:

- Come prepared. Most meetings have a written agenda. Know ahead of time what your role will be. If you need to make a report, know ahead of time what you will say.

Today's Meeting Agenda

Directions:	For each meeting you attend, write down the agenda or study the written agenda before the meeting begins.

*Today's agenda: Carson Management Report,
3rd Quarter Sales Projections, Health Insurance Rate Increase*

Notes for My Presentation

Directions: Write down ahead of time the key points you wish to make in your presentation.

Sample 1: *Sales are up 5 percent*

Sample 2: *Keep momentum up*

Sample 3: *Sales campaign in Peoria will start next week*

1.

2.

3.

4.

5.

• If you have a choice in seating, be close enough to the speaker that you can easily hear him. Choose a seat that allows you to assess the speaker's body language and maintain eye contact. Remember it is difficult to have eye contact with those seated on either side of you.

- Just because others in the meeting may be poor listeners, don't stop using Active Listening yourself. Ask questions to clarify participants' positions. If the meeting starts to wander, ask questions designed to get the speaker or others back on track.

- Know your priorities before you go into the meeting so you can listen actively. For example, if you are going to be asked to voice your opinion about a decision, having your priorities in order will help you actively listen to what others are saying. What do you want to accomplish during the meeting?

Priorities for Today's Meeting

Directions: List your priorities for today's meeting.

1.

2.

3.

4.

5.

- If the speaker says something that upsets you, control your emotions. Avoid any emotionally charged exchanges. Count to 10 and then respond. When finished, consciously do an awareness check of your emotional and mental filters. What caused you to react that way?

Review Questions:

1. What does LLAMA stand for?

2. How do your filters affect your listening?

3. How do your boss's filters affect your listening?

4. What are the five effective steps to communicating with your boss?

5. What role do you play as an employee?

6. How does that role affect listening effectively to those who manage you?

7. How does the role you play affect listening effectively to your co-workers?

8. What percentage of the time should you spend listening and talking?

9. How do the emotional filters of those you manage affect their ability to listen to you?

Other Business Listening Situations

Listening to your manager, co-workers and those you manage will take up the majority of your workday. However, there are other business listening situations where practicing Active Listening is also useful.

Listening in Boring Meetings

Time-consuming meetings are a necessary evil in the business world. It cannot function without them. Using Active Listening can make a meeting more productive for you. If the meeting is boring, try these techniques:

- As you listen, identify the points that directly affect you. This will become your "to do" list after the meeting.

> *"The man who lets himself be bored is even more contemptible than the bore."*
>
> *Samuel Butler*

217

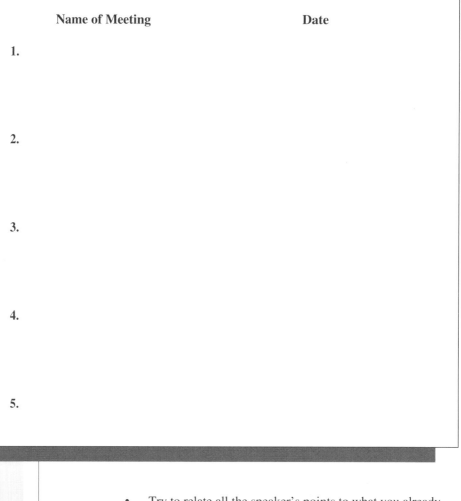

Meeting Worksheet

Directions: List the points that affect you from the meetings below.

	Name of Meeting	Date
1.		
2.		
3.		
4.		
5.		

- Try to relate all the speaker's points to what you already know about the topic or situation. For example, if the speaker is droning on about the quality-control crisis in the company, relate what he is saying to what you know about quality control and how it affects your department.

Points That I Can Relate to Because of Prior Knowledge About the Topic

Directions: List the points made in the meeting that you can relate to because you have previous knowledge about the topic.

1. *Understood Malthusian Theory*

2.

3.

4.

5.

- Ask questions that show you have been listening but that also force the speaker to stick to the agenda and stay focused. For example, if the speaker rambles on about the upcoming Christmas party when the topic is December's production quota, ask him a question such as, "What will my department's quota be for December?"

• Take notes to focus your attention.

Following is an example of note-taking that is commonly taught. The concept is relatively simple. In the right column, you take notes on the meeting. In the left column, you list key words or concepts related to the notes on the right. The key words and concepts act as both an outline and a quick way of reviewing the high points of the meeting. The notes give you the details needed.

Sample Note-taking Format	
Key Words/Concepts	**Notes from Meeting**
Contract	*Negotiations continue. Management reluctant to increase wages. Mediation may be necessary.*

- If all else fails and you can't get the speaker back on the topic, or if he just drones on and on, send nonverbal signals that you are bored. For example, you could move around in your chair restlessly. You could start to organize your papers in front of you. Use this type of behavior judiciously, especially if the speaker is your boss.

Listening to a Lecture

On occasion you will need to listen to a lecture in either a work or an educational environment. Here are some tips on getting the most out of a lecture using Active Listening.

- Sit near the front so that you have a clear view of the speaker and his body language. For some, body language reinforces the speaker's words and helps them remember what the speaker said. It's also harder to be inattentive if you are at the front of an audience. If you sit in the back, you will be distracted by all the people sitting in front of you.

- Come to the lecture prepared. Ask yourself, "What's in it for me?" Review what you already know about the subject so you can relate the lecture to your interests. This technique will help you get more out of the lecture.

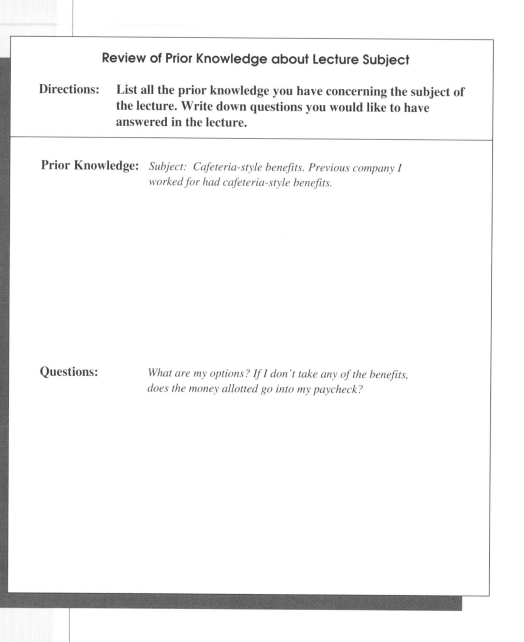

Review of Prior Knowledge about Lecture Subject

Directions: **List all the prior knowledge you have concerning the subject of the lecture. Write down questions you would like to have answered in the lecture.**

Prior Knowledge: *Subject: Cafeteria-style benefits. Previous company I worked for had cafeteria-style benefits.*

Questions: *What are my options? If I don't take any of the benefits, does the money allotted go into my paycheck?*

• Take notes, but do not try to write down everything. Don't be consumed by your notes; record essential points only. Too many notes will distract you from the full message.

- Go into the lecture with high expectations. You hear what you expect to hear. If you think the lecture will be boring, it probably will be.

- Look attentive. Send positive body-language signals to the speaker. Lean forward, for example. Smile. Encourage the speaker and he probably will give a better lecture.

Listening in Interviews

Key Idea:

If you're a poor listener and you're interviewing someone, you may end up hiring the wrong person. If you're a poor listener and you are being interviewed, you may blow your chances at a job because of inappropriate responses or poor nonverbal communication. Here are some techniques to improve your listening in either situation.

Listening Techniques If You Are the Interviewer:

- Ask open-ended questions. Then use Active Listening to assess the response of the person being interviewed. For example, you set up a situation and then ask, "How would you handle this situation?" Then listen for his verbal and nonverbal response.

- Use Reflective Listening if you are unsure of a response. Repeating what the person has just said can help you clarify. The interviewee says, "My last job allowed me to leave work on Friday when I was finished." To clarify you would say, "I understand you saying that you could leave anytime on Fridays if your work was done."

"There is nothing harder than the softness of indifference."

Juan Montalvo

Reflective Listening Exercise

Directions: How would you respond to the following statements made by a person being interviewed? Use questions or statements that show that you are listening reflectively.

1. "My last boss was such a jerk."

   Sample: *"I hear you saying you were unhappy with the performance of your boss."*

2. "I was fired for the silliest reason."

3. "I'm sure I could learn."

4. "I'm really worried about what I've heard about this company."

- Use nonverbal communication to put the person at ease. Smile. Sit in a relaxed manner rather than appearing tense.

- Pay close attention to the nonverbal communication of the person being interviewed. His nonverbal communication, which is emotionally based, may give you more information about him than his verbal responses, which are intellectually based. Does he look nervous? Is he mirroring your nonverbals, which would indicate he's in agreement with you? Is he smiling?

Listening Techniques if You Are Being Interviewed:

- Monitor and control your nonverbal communication so you send a consistent message to the interviewer. For example, if you are tense and uptight about the interview, practice a relaxation technique such as deep breathing.

Eloquence:
Saying the
proper thing and
stopping.

Practice in Monitoring Nonverbal Communication

Directions: Practice answering interview questions in front of a mirror.
Note your nonverbal communication. Is it sending a consistent
message? Use the following questions.

1. Describe the duties you performed in your last position.

2. What kind of employee are you and why do you describe yourself that
way?

3. Tell me something about your educational background.

4. It has been said that we learn the most from our mistakes. What
mistakes have you made in the past, and what have you learned from
them?

5. Where do you see yourself in 10 years?

- Mirroring the interviewer's body language shows that you are in agreement. For example, if the interviewer crosses his left leg over his right, cross your right leg over your left. This mirrors his body language.

- Use Active and Reflective Listening. If you understand only part of a question, use Reflective Listening techniques to seek clarification before you answer. If the interviewer says, "Your workweek will run from Monday through Sunday," and you're not sure what that means, you could say, "I hear you saying that I would work seven days a week. Is that correct?"

- Maintain eye contact while you are listening. This shows that you are interested in what the interviewer says. This technique could help you land a new job.

- If you have control over where you sit, place yourself so that you can assess the interviewer's nonverbal communication. Try to eliminate any physical barriers between you and the interviewer. This may be difficult since most interviews are conducted from behind a desk or at a table.

Listening in Sales

Listening is absolutely essential in the sales field. If you don't listen, you can't close the sale because you won't know what the customer wants. You may even make a mistake in the customer's order if you're not listening. People often buy for emotional reasons if they believe the product or service will help them in some way. They want to have their needs met. Obviously, listening will help you make the sale because you will hear what the customer's needs are.

> *"Better to remain silent and be thought a fool than to speak out and remove all doubt."*
>
> *Abraham Lincoln*

C
L
O
S
E

Following is a memory device for salespeople suggested by Jim Cairo in his audiotapes, *The Power of Effective Listening*.

C	=	**Concentrate**
L	=	**Listen**
O	=	**Open listening**
S	=	**Suspend judgments**
E	=	**Empathize**

By using this system, you will close more sales. Here's how it works.

C = Concentrate. Since you usually can't control the selling environment, you will need to concentrate and also get the buyer to concentrate on your sales pitch. Try to eliminate as many barriers as possible in the environment. If you meet your prospective clients in their homes, for example, try to choose a place where they can see your product or materials to your best advantage. Politely ask them to turn off or turn down the television or radio.

L = Listen. Using Active Listening you can better understand the buyer's needs. You should talk 20 percent of the time and listen the remaining 80 percent.

O = Open listening. Keep your mind open to what the customer is saying. Assess the nonverbals of the buyer and be aware of the message you are sending with your nonverbals.

S = Suspend judgments. The buyer's opinions are important. This is no time for a debate. Listen carefully and without judgment to his needs.

E = Empathize. Show you care by actively and reflectively listening. Nobody wants to buy from someone who does not seem to care about his needs. If he talks about his concerns about his daughter's education, respond with empathy.

Taking time to follow these steps with a potential customer will usually result in a sale.

My Action Plan for Improving Listening in My Sales:

Goals to Accomplish:

Obstacles Keeping Me from Accomplishing These Goals:

Steps to Accomplish These Goals:

Time Line for Accomplishing These Goals:

Telephone Listening

Listening on the telephone may constitute a large part of your day. You are at somewhat of a disadvantage when listening on the phone because you cannot see the person you are speaking to and consequently cannot assess his body language. However, there are some techniques you can use to maximize your telephone listening.

- Control the telephone. Don't let it control you. Answer it when you are ready. Take the phone off the hook or ask for your calls to be taken. Use your answering machine. Just because the phone rings, you don't have to answer it.

- Control your environment so that you can concentrate on the speaker. Close your door or ask others in the area to be quiet if necessary.

- Listen for content and intent. Nonverbals such as pitch, tone and rate become important. Make your voice "smile."

- Practice good body language while on the phone. It will be conveyed through your voice.

- Practice Active as well as Reflective Listening.

Summary

Active and Reflective Listening can improve your communication at work and in many business-related situations. The techniques are easy, immediate and applicable. To be a more effective listener, you don't need to be an expert. You only have to be willing to try.

Review Questions:

1. Which techniques for listening in meetings have you tried? Were they successful?

2. Which listening techniques are important when conducting an interview? When being interviewed?

3. What does the memory device CLOSE stand for?

4. How can you increase your effectiveness in listening on the telephone?

CHAPTER 12

Personal Listening Situations

Listening to those you live with or care deeply for is important. Unfortunately, most of us don't practice Active Listening in these situations, yet that is precisely what can make or break a relationship. With business associates, you may have to take time to get to know them in order to practice Active Listening. But with family members, you already know their backgrounds. In many cases, the same is true with your friends. The longer you have known someone, the easier it should be to actively listen to him or her. However, that is not always the case. The saying,

> ### "Familiarity breeds contempt."

could just as easily say,

> ### "Familiarity breeds barriers to Active Listening."

"Other things may change us, but we start and end with family."

Anthony Brandt

Sometimes familiarity means that you take the other person for granted.

Personal Listening Questions

Directions: Answer the following questions about your own listening in personal situations.

1. When was the last time you really listened to what your husband, wife or significant other was saying?

2. When was the last time you really heard what your children were saying?

3. When was the last time you really heard what your friends were saying?

4. When was the last time you really heard what your parents were saying?

5. Do you interpret what they all say based on your own personal listening filters or hidden agenda?

Most of us hear, few of us listen. It's a wonder more families don't break up or that we have any friends at all!

Four Guidelines to Better Listening with Family and Friends

Follow these steps to really listen to your family and friends:

1. Identify the kind of listening you use with your family and friends.

2. Recognize your personal listening pitfalls.

3. Know your family and friends.

4. Put Active Listening into effect.

Listening in Social Situations

Most listening in social situations takes place on a one-on-one basis or in small groups. Even though social situations are often composed of small talk, they need not be. With Active and Reflective Listening you can move the conversation into more interesting areas. Try these points at the next cocktail party or social function.

- Ask open-ended questions and then sit back and listen. People love to talk about themselves. The best open-ended question is "Tell me about your work (or family)."

Open-Ended Questions to Use in a Social Situation

1.   Tell me about your work.

2.   Tell me about your family.

3.   What do you think about...?

4.   I just heard the most interesting idea. What do you think about it?

Directions: Now write some open-ended questions or statements of your own that could be used in a social situation.

1.

2.

3.

4.

- Use Reflective Listening if the conversation turns to a controversial problem that you don't want to debate. For example, if at a social gathering your host says, "The Supreme Court should reverse its stand on abortion," answer reflectively by saying, "I understand you don't agree with the Supreme Court in this issue."

- Use your body language to show that you are listening. Remember that mirroring the speaker's body language shows that you are in agreement with him.

- Avoid conflict by listening with empathy and without judging. Though you may not agree with what he is saying, you don't have to argue with him. Remember this is a social situation, not a debate.

- Use your listening skills to break away from a boring person. Introduce him to someone else by asking him to tell the new person about whatever you have been talking about. Then politely excuse yourself.

> *"Well-timed silence has more eloquence than speech."*
>
> *Sophie Tucker*

My Action Plan to Improve Listening in a Social Situation

Goals to Accomplish:

Obstacles Keeping Me from Accomplishing These Goals:

Steps to Accomplish These Goals:

Time Line for Accomplishing These Goals:

Friends

You may already have a reputation as a good listener among your friends. You are probably confused about how you got that reputation. It's easy enough. Whether you realize it or not, you have been actively listening. You have been sending the message that you care and that you're not going to judge someone just by what he says. What more could a friend ask for?

Identify the kind of listening you use with your friends.

Your best and oldest friends are the ones that you have actively listened to the most. When building a new friendship you are more likely to fall back into Selective Listening and Passive Listening. It's probably because you don't know your new friends very well yet.

Listening to My Friends

Directions: Indicate below how often you use each type of listening with your friends.

	Always	Sometimes	Never
Active	❑	❑	❑
Selective	❑	❑	❑
Reflective	❑	❑	❑
Poor (filled with emotional/mental filters)	❑	❑	❑

Recognize Your Personal Listening Pitfalls

These will be similar to your listening pitfalls with business associates. They include specific words, actions, and ideas or topics that send you a red flag. Your listening filters put up a barrier to them. For example, you may get embarrassed when someone brings up the topic of alcoholism and, therefore, have trouble listening because your father was an alcoholic.

Personal Listening Pitfalls with My Friends

Directions: **List words, actions, ideas and topics used by your friends that affect your listening.**

Wendy always uses the term "redneck" and I have trouble listening to whom she's talking about.

Know Your Friends

The more you know about your friends, the better you will be equipped to actively listen to them. This does not mean that you need to be a gossip or snoop. You should respect their privacy and understand that what they tell you in confidence should not be repeated.

Put Active Listening into Effect

Once you have followed the previous steps, you are ready to put Active Listening into effect.

Listening to Your Children

Actively Listening to your children is extremely important if you hope to make clear and open communication a habit. How many times have you heard teenagers say, "My parents just don't understand me!!" Also, you provide a model of behavior for your children, so teach them Active Listening skills by example.

Often when children want you to listen to them, they communicate this need nonverbally. Children's body language is a good barometer of how they feel and whether they need to be listened to. A 3-year-old—all teary-eyed—needs someone to take some time to listen to him. A teenager sulking in his room is sending the same message—"listen to me."

Techniques for Listening to Children:

- The younger the child, the more you will need to "listen" to his body language and then ask carefully phrased questions to find out what the problem is.

  Example: Instead of asking your teary-eyed 3-year-old who comes running into the house, "Did that big, bad dog scare you?" say, "Are you crying because something scared you?" If he says, "Yes," then ask, "What was it?" If he doesn't know, then it's 20 Questions time. If you initially suggest to him that the dog scared him and it didn't, then you've introduced another topic to deal with and you may never find out what really scared him.

> *"The greatest act of love is to pay attention ... I think the one lesson I have learned is that there is no substitute for paying attention."*
>
> *Diane Sawyer*

241

Analysis of a Recent Situation in Which I Could Have Listened and Communicated Better with a Younger Child

Directions: List a recent situation in which you could have listened more carefully and communicated better with a younger child. List the questions you could have asked.

Situation	Questions I Could Have Asked
My 4-year-old's nightmare	*Can you tell me what you saw in your dream?*

- Listen for "my friend" statements. Quite often a child will describe his problem by talking about a friend who has the same problem. For example, your son may say, "My friend doesn't know what to do. His best friend is angry with him and my friend wants to punch him." More than likely your child is talking about himself.

- Be prepared to listen to fantasy friends. Speaking through your child, they can give you a lot of information about your child's fears and concerns. For example, if your daughter's fantasy friend is Tina, questions about Tina may give you insight into your daughter's feelings.

- Use Reflective Listening to help your child clarify and understand his problems. This is more appropriate when the child is older. A child often is trying to understand how he stands on issues. Reflective Listening can help him do that. If he says, "Mr. Julius really ticked me off. He says I was cheating on the math test and I wasn't. I was only asking for a pencil." You could reflectively answer, "I hear you saying that you don't think Mr. Julius made a fair decision because he didn't have all the information." This restates what the child has said and allows him to work through his feelings about the problem.

"No one ever keeps a secret so well as a child."

Victor Hugo

Analysis of a Recent Situation in Which I Could Have Used Reflective Listening with an Older Child

Directions: Analyze a recent situation in which you could have used Reflective Listening with an older child but didn't. What questions could you have used that would have helped the child?

Situation	Questions I Could Have Asked
Mandy's fight with Jeff	*Is it possible that Jeff feels badly too?*

- Monitor your nonverbal communication so it doesn't send conflicting signals to your child. For example, if you are trying to show that you are concerned, don't frown at what your child is saying.

Nonverbals I Use with My Child

Directions: List below those nonverbal signals you send when listening to your child. What message do those nonverbals send?

Nonverbal	**Message It Sends**
Frown	*That I'm unhappy with him*

Are your nonverbal signals sending the message you want to send? If not, how can you change them?

- By listening in an empathic and nonjudgmental way, you will get more information from your child. This does not mean that you have to accept everything he tells you. Suspend judgment until you hear the whole story. If you judge immediately, he'll clam up and communication will stop.

Case Study:

Your daughter comes home in tears and says, "I don't know why Mr. Morgan hates me so much. He showed Becky the list of starters for the basketball team and she said I'm not on it. I just know he doesn't like me." She throws her books down on the sofa and runs to her room crying. You follow to help her.

Case Study Analysis:

Whose problem is this? Your daughter's, but as a parent you may want to make it your problem. Instead, if you listen reflectively, you will help her understand and deal with the problem herself. Use a feeling message. When you use a feeling message, it's a good idea to give yourself time to think. Ask yourself, "What is my daughter feeling?" and "Why is she feeling this way?" The formula for a feeling message is "You feel _____ because _____ _____."

You are reflecting back the feelings and the reasons for the feelings as you understand them. Your response might be "You feel hurt because your name was not on the basketball list" or "You feel Mr. Morgan hates you because your name wasn't on the list." Feeling messages help clarify emotional statements. The key to feeling messages is that you don't become emotional yourself. Check your feelings. If you're emotional, then you're not listening reflectively.

Listening to Your Teenager

Probably a whole book could be written about listening to your teenager. As your child becomes older, Active Listening becomes more and more important. Listening to younger children helps them build their self-esteem and understand your values and expectations. Listening to your teenager helps you and your child survive the sometimes traumatic teen years.

C A S E   S T U D Y

> The two most important points of listening to your teenager are:
>
> 1. **Listen with empathy and without judgment.**
>
> 2. **Listen reflectively.**

C A S E   S T U D Y

Naturally, all the other techniques of Active Listening are important, but if you can achieve these two, then you have a chance at keeping communication open with your teen.

Listening with Empathy and Without Judgment

This is essential in listening to teenagers. By nature they are stretching their wings, trying to break away. At times, both their actions and their words are hard for you to accept. Many times they do and say things just to get a reaction. If you listen with empathy, you send the message that you care about them, no matter how they look or sound based on your values. If you listen without judging, you send the message that you are suspending judgment until they have a chance to explain themselves. You are willing to listen to them. This is important in their quest for independence.

Case Study:

Maria, your 16-year-old, uncharacteristically slams her books on the table as she enters the kitchen. You ask, "Is there anything wrong?", to which she answers, "I don't care if I ever see Jared again." You personally don't care for Jared, though you have heard that he isn't so bad once you get past his appearance. You're afraid to ask Maria if she's been secretly dating Jared, but at the same time it's so unlike Maria to be this upset. You know that something is wrong and she needs someone to listen.

Which of the following do you say?

A. "I suppose the creep Jared's been at it again."

B. "Would you like to talk about it?"

C. "When you're so angry that you slam books, I get worried. Does this have to do with Jared?"

You might be tempted to say response A because that's the way you feel about Jared. However, if Maria has been dating Jared, using the word "creep" may make her side with Jared, no matter what he did to her. You might want to say response B because it seems like a valid question, but in reality you may get the one-word answer, "No." Then the discussion is closed. Response C is best because it shows your concern, but doesn't judge Maria or Jared.

Listen Reflectively

Once you have listened with empathy and without passing judgment, use Reflective Listening to help teenagers understand what they are saying. It is better for them to come to grips with their ideas, words and actions themselves than for you to explain or judge them. Reflective Listening helps teenagers make decisions, shows them they are cared for and loved, and it keeps communication lines open. Reflective Listening also takes the burden of being the bad guy off your shoulders.

Case Study:

Your son Lamont and your daughter Linda, 13 and 15 years old, respectively, are arguing at the dinner table. Linda says, "Mr. Miller is so unfair. In math today he called on me and embarrassed me."

"You're crazy. Mr. Miller's the best math teacher at Coolidge."

"Says you. He's just a chauvinist. He loves to call on the girls to prove that girls aren't as smart as boys."

C
A
S
E

S
T
U
D
Y

"He's right there," says Lamont.

"Just because you brown-nose him doesn't mean he's good."

"Dad! Make her take back what she said!"

At this point, clarification of the issues rather than escalation of the war seems in order. Which of the following questions should you use to help your teenagers clarify what they are talking about?

A.   What did Mr. Miller do to embarrass you?

B.   Is Mr. Miller really a chauvinist?

C.   I hear you saying Mr. Miller is a chauvinist, Linda. What makes you think that?

D.   Why can't you get good math grades like your brother?

When listening reflectively, response C is the appropriate choice. It tells your teenager you hear what she is saying and asks her to clarify her position. Notice, it does not judge her statement.

Listening to Your Spouse

Listening to your spouse is extremely important. One of the most important reasons given for the breakdown of a marriage is, "My spouse doesn't listen to me anymore." Stable relationships are built on effective listening skills. Like listening to teenagers, a whole book could be written about listening to your spouse. But the No. 1 strategy for listening to your spouse is:

Listen with empathy and without judgment.

Although it seems obvious, many people fail to take the time and energy to practice Active Listening. Listening with empathy sends the message that you care about your spouse and that you understand how he or she is feeling. This understanding alone is enough to improve a shaky relationship.

By listening to your spouse in a nonjudgmental way, you show respect for your spouse's ideas—that you see them as having equal value to your own. This, too, helps because a good relationship is built on respect.

Analysis of How I Listen to My Spouse

Directions: Circle the response that best describes how you listen to your spouse.

| **Very Well** | **Well** | **All Right** | **Not So Well** | **Terrible** |

Why did you mark the answer that you did?

What can you do to improve the way you listen to your spouse?

Try These Techniques When Listening to Your Spouse:

- Put aside what you are doing when your spouse wants to talk. Give him or her your complete attention. Having a conversation about your son's school problems is difficult if one of you is listening to the football game or reading the newspaper.

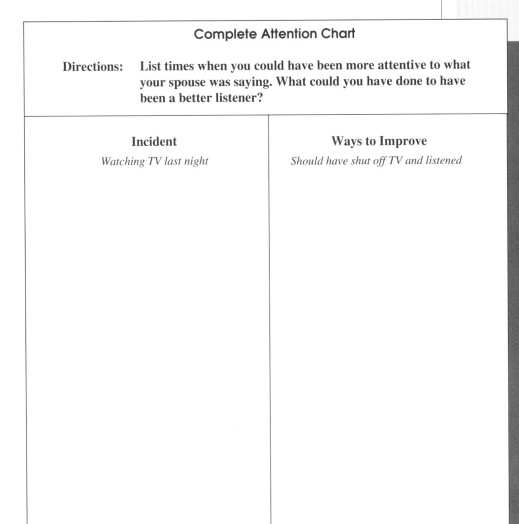

Complete Attention Chart

Directions: List times when you could have been more attentive to what your spouse was saying. What could you have done to have been a better listener?

Incident	Ways to Improve
Watching TV last night	*Should have shut off TV and listened*

- Listen with your whole body. Maintain eye contact. Move forward. Send positive "I'm-listening-to-you" messages with your body language.

- Control your emotions. Since your spouse probably knows you as well as, if not better than, anyone else, he or she recognizes your "hot buttons." Do not react if he or she is angry and tries to irritate you by pushing them. If your spouse says, "Your mother's trying to control our lives again," and your mother is one of your hot buttons, don't overreact. Use Reflective Listening. Say, "I hear you saying my mother's interfering again."

"Hot Buttons" That Affect Listening to My Spouse

Directions: **List below those "hot buttons" that affect effectively listening to your spouse.**

Mentioning my weekly night out with friends

- If your spouse is upset, use Reflective Listening to help him or her work out the problem. Your spouse does not necessarily want you to solve the problem, but does want you to listen to the problem, provide support and react to feelings and ideas. For example, your spouse says, "I'm sick and tired of being the only one who does any work around here." Your reflective response is, "You feel like you're the only one who does any work at home."

Key Idea:

Listen to your spouse the way you would want him to listen to you.

Recognize your personal listening pitfalls.

At the beginning of a relationship, recognizing your personal listening pitfalls is important because you want to understand what your new boyfriend or girlfriend is communicating. Since there is so much to learn about each other, you constantly re-evaluate yourself in relationship to him or her. For example, in just one week you discover that your boyfriend likes to drive fast cars, listen to Italian opera at full volume and can't stand eggs, your favorite food. If you practice Active Listening, you will increase your knowledge about the person. Your ability to Actively Listen to him or her will become easier and easier with this knowledge.

With marriage or living together, Active Listening becomes more important as you continue to build a relationship. The newness of living together opens new areas of communication. By living together, you discover facets of your partner's personality you didn't know existed. For example, you discover that he is a neatnik when it comes to the bathroom but doesn't hear you when you ask him not to leave his underwear in the living room. If Active Listening is not practiced, the relationship may be off to a rocky start.

After you have been living together for some time, you may fall into the comfortableness of the relationship. This can lead to hearing rather than listening to what your partner is saying because of the predictability of your relationship. For instance, some couples have heard each other's stories so many times they could just as well call them Story # 1 or Story # 5 rather than repeat the story again. As time goes on, you no longer hang on every word your

253

partner says. You have lapsed into predictable listening. You're not even being selective anymore. You just know what your partner is going to say. This is a dangerous stage that can be characterized by one of the biggest complaints of unhappily married couples, "He (or she) never listens to me any more."

Predictable Listening Situations

Directions: **List your partner's stories or phrases that you have heard enough times that you just "turn them off."**

My husband's story about getting rid of the rabid cat

There are ways to combat predictable listening. Try some of these techniques.

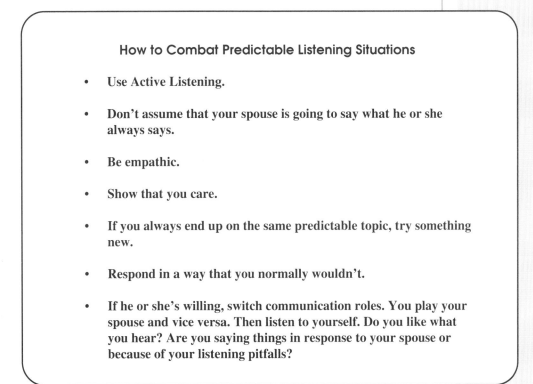

How to Combat Predictable Listening Situations

- **Use Active Listening.**

- **Don't assume that your spouse is going to say what he or she always says.**

- **Be empathic.**

- **Show that you care.**

- **If you always end up on the same predictable topic, try something new.**

- **Respond in a way that you normally wouldn't.**

- **If he or she's willing, switch communication roles. You play your spouse and vice versa. Then listen to yourself. Do you like what you hear? Are you saying things in response to your spouse or because of your listening pitfalls?**

Parents

As you become an adult, you realize that your parents probably still see you as a child. They may continue to treat you and communicate with you as if you're stuck at some magical age. However, by practicing Active Listening, you may be able to get unstuck and forge ahead into an adult relationship with your parents.

Identify the kind of listening you use with your parents.

If your relationship with your parents is good, you are probably already using Active Listening. For many adults and their parents, Selective Listening is as good as it gets.

"Reverence for parents stands written among the three laws of most revered righteousness."

Aeschylus

Look for These Signs of Active Listening to Your Parents:

1. You listen to the content of what your parents say. You listen to their words.

2. You listen to the intent of what your parents say. You are aware of what they are saying because of their nonverbal communication, both body language and tone of voice.

3. You analyze their nonverbal communication and put it in the context of your parents' personalities, personal backgrounds and cultures. For example, since your father grew up in Norway, you have come to expect him to show little emotion. He holds it in, because that is what he was taught to do as a child. If he smiles slightly, you take it as immense approval of what was said.

4. You listen in an empathic and nonjudgmental way. Your body language sends the message that you care about your parents.

5. You respond to your parents with "I" messages and non-judgmental statements.

Look for These Signs of Selective Listening to Your Parents:

1. You listen to the content of what your parents say.

2. You are aware of the intent of what your parents say by their nonverbal communication.

3. You respond emotionally to your parents when you agree with them.

Look for These Signs of Passive Listening to Your Parents:

1. You hear the content of what your parents say.

2. You are aware sometimes of the intent of what your parents say by their nonverbal communication.

3. You sometimes respond emotionally to your parents' communication, and other times you do not respond at all.

You may, of course, respond differently to each parent. For example, you may actively listen to your father but passively listen to your mother.

Parental Listening Chart

Directions: Check below the type of listening you use most often with each of your parents. List in the space provided when you are most likely to use this kind of listening.

	Active	Selective	Passive
Father	❑	❑	❑
Times			
Mother	❑	❑	❑
Times			
Stepfather	❑	❑	❑
Times			
Stepmother	❑	❑	❑
Times			

Recognize your personal listening pitfalls.

Usually you have known your parents longer than anyone else. For the most part, they have influenced you, molded you and taught you how to listen. If you have disagreements with your parents that have never been resolved, you will have a personal listening pitfall until the issues are put to rest.

Almost every family has a topic that is "taboo." All you have to do is attend a family reunion. Invariably, someone will bring up the forbidden topic, usually an innocent person who married into the family. Once the topic is introduced, feathers are ruffled or worse. More than likely, these taboo topics were originally disagreements between family members. To actively listen to your parents, you need to identify those topics, words, ideas and even commands or expectations that impede communicating with them at an adult level. Perhaps they always treat you like you are 10 years old. Maybe you feel they think you are irresponsible. Maybe you've never forgiven them for taking away your car the day before prom. Identifying these pitfalls will help eliminate filters that get in the way of really listening to what your parents are saying.

"Hot Buttons" That Affect Listening to My Parents

Directions: List the topics, ideas, and words that affect listening to your parents.

My involvement in the Democratic party when they are long-time Republicans

Know your parents.

Knowing your parents can be as hard as knowing your children. After all, what you know the most about them is how they act as parents. Now that you are an adult, you need to sort out your feelings about them. Separate their behavior as a parent from their other behaviors. You may be surprised to find that you like your father as an adult, but you didn't like him when you were growing up. Knowing who they are will help you actively listen to them as adults, rather than as parents. It will also help you separate when they are speaking in the parental voice from when they are speaking in their adult voice.

> *"Old people love to give good advice; it compensates them for their inability to set a bad example."*
>
> *La Rochefoucauld*

Listening to TV

Another type of listening comes into play when you watch television. Obviously, you do not respond to television as you would to a fellow worker or family member, because television is passive. However, that doesn't mean that you shouldn't use Active Listening. All of the steps in Active Listening can be used with television except asking questions for clarification and for Reflective Listening. Listening for content, intent and nonverbals are all possible. For example, when you watch a talk show, actively listen to what the person being interviewed says. Listen for his content, intent and nonverbals.

Listening to Yourself

Self-talk is a popular concept, and it can be very effective. Equally important is your ability to listen to what you are saying to others. Do you actually mean what you say? Are your nonverbals consistent with what you are saying? Do you say things like "I could just kill you" when you mean you're angry? What message does that give to your family and friends? Are you constantly using negative tones or phrases out of habit and not because you are really negative? Listen to what you say. You might be surprised.

Inventory of What I Say

Directions: List below those nonverbal signals and common expressions that you consistently use. You may have to ask a close friend or family member to help you identify them. Then analyze those nonverbals.

What My Nonverbals Say/ What Common Expressions I Use:
"You're kidding!" with a surprised look

The Nature of My Intent:
Excitement about others' ideas

Ways I Can Change My Communication to Say What I Really Mean:
Verbally say, "I like your idea."

Summary

Listening is important not only in business but also in personal situations. If you can become an effective listener in your personal life, your listening in business situations will also improve.

Review Questions:

1. What techniques have you learned to improve your listening in social situations?

2. What techniques have you learned to improve listening to your children?

3. What techniques have you learned to improve listening to your spouse?

4. How can you use the tips in this chapter to improve listening to your parents?

C *HAPTER 13*

Conclusion

Throughout this book, you've learned how to improve your listening skills. These techniques are summed up by Jim Cairo in his tapes, *The Power of Effective Listening.* Here are his rules or commandments for good listening.

Ten Rules for Good Listening

1. **Be motivated to listen.**
2. **Care about the speaker and show it.**
3. **Use all of your physical being to show that you are a good listener. Use body language.**
4. **Use all of your senses to determine another's meaning.**
5. **Strive for accuracy.**
6. **Do not judge.**
7. **Control the listening situation.**
8. **Increase your power of retention through observation.**
9. **Practice good listening and teach good listening.**
10. **Listen to yourself.**

To see if you've already put some of these techniques into practice, take this final listening survey.

Final Listening Survey

Directions: Using a scale of 1 to 10, rate yourself on each of the 10 rules of good listening — 1 is the lowest, 10 the highest.

1. I am motivated to listen.   1 2 3 4 5 6 7 8 9 10

2. I care about the speaker and show it.   1 2 3 4 5 6 7 8 9 10

3. I use all of my physical being to show
    that I am a good listener.   1 2 3 4 5 6 7 8 9 10

4. I use all of my senses to determine
    another's meaning.   1 2 3 4 5 6 7 8 9 10

5. I strive for accuracy.   1 2 3 4 5 6 7 8 9 10

6. I do not judge.   1 2 3 4 5 6 7 8 9 10

7. I control the listening situation.   1 2 3 4 5 6 7 8 9 10

8. I increase my power of retention
    through observation.   1 2 3 4 5 6 7 8 9 10

9. I practice good listening and
    teach good listening.   1 2 3 4 5 6 7 8 9 10

10. I listen to myself.   1 2 3 4 5 6 7 8 9 10

Final Listening Survey (Continued)

Directions: Add up the numbers you circled.

Key:

10-30 — You are a poor listener. You definitely need to work on your listening skills.

31-51 — You are at the low end of average listening. You need to work on your listening skills.

51-70 — You are at the high end of average listening. You need some work on your listening skills.

71-100 — You are a good listener. Keep up the good work!

Don't be discouraged if your score didn't meet your expectations. Just the fact that you care enough about improving your listening to read this book is a real accomplishment. You'll be surprised by the number of listening techniques you've already picked up. Remember, listening is something you practice countless times each day. Using this book as a guide, you're guaranteed to see and hear improvement.

*I*NDEX

Other Training Resources Available From National Press Publications

Desktop Handbooks

National Press Publications Desktop Handbooks take the essentials of an important subject and distill them into a focused, concise handbook that's short (no more than 120 pages), easy to use and convenient. Their durable spiral binding allows them to lie flat on your desktop and the high-quality manufacture means they'll stay with you all the way to the boardroom. The books in this series have sold more than a million copies for one simple reason – people recognize outstanding quality and value when they see it. Each book is a gold mine of instant information you'll turn to again and again. We guarantee it!

The Leadership Series

Qty.	Item#	Title	U.S.	Can.	Total
	410	The Supervisor's Handbook, Revised and Expanded	$12.95	$14.95	
	458	Positive Performance Management: *A Guide to Win-Win Reviews*	$12.95	$14.95	
	459	Techniques of Successful Delegation	$12.95	$14.95	
	463	Powerful Leadership Skills for Women	$12.95	$14.95	
	469	Peak Performance	$12.95	$14.95	
	494	Team-Building	$12.95	$14.95	
	495	How to Manage Conflict	$12.95	$14.95	
	418	Total Quality Management	$12.95	$14.95	

The Communication Series

	413	Dynamic Communication Skills for Women	$12.95	$14.95	
	414	The Write Stuff: *A Style Manual for Effective Business Writing*	$12.95	$14.95	
	417	Listen Up: *Hear What's Really Being Said*	$12.95	$14.95	
	442	Assertiveness: *Get What You Want Without Being Pushy*	$12.95	$14.95	
	460	Techniques to Improve Your Writing Skills	$12.95	$14.95	
	461	Powerful Presentation Skills	$12.95	$14.95	
	482	Techniques of Effective Telephone Communication	$12.95	$14.95	
	485	Personal Negotiating Skills	$12.95	$14.95	
	488	Customer Service: *The Key to Winning Lifetime Customers*	$12.95	$14.95	
	498	How to Manage Your Boss	$12.95	$14.95	

The Productivity Series

	411	Getting Things Done: *An Achiever's Guide to Time Management*	$12.95	$14.95	
	443	A New Attitude	$12.95	$14.95	
	468	Understanding the Bottom Line: *Finance for the Non-Financial Manager*	$12.95	$14.95	
	483	Successful Sales Strategies: *A Woman's Perspective*	$12.95	$14.95	
	489	Doing Business Over the Phone: *Telemarketing for the '90s*	$12.95	$14.95	
	496	Motivation & Goal-Setting: *The Keys to Achieving Success*	$12.95	$14.95	

Desktop Handbooks continued

The Lifestyle Series

Qty.	Item#	Title	U.S.	Can.	Total
	415	Balancing Career & Family: *Overcoming the Superwoman Syndrome*	$12.95	$14.95	
	416	Real Men Don't Vacuum	$12.95	$14.95	
	464	Self-Esteem: *The Power to Be Your Best*	$12.95	$14.95	
	484	The Stress Management Handbook	$12.95	$14.95	
	486	Parenting: *Ward & June Don't Live Here Anymore*	$12.95	$14.95	
	487	How to Get the Job You Want	$12.95	$14.95	

Business User's Manuals

Qty.	Item#	Title	U.S.	Can.	Total
	447	To Meet or Not to Meet: *How to Plan and Conduct Effective Meetings*	$24.95	$28.95	
	449	Business Letters for Busy People	$24.95	$28.95	
	451	Think Like a Manager	$24.95	$28.95	
	452	The Memory System	$24.95	$28.95	
	453	Prioritize ... Organize ... *The Art of Getting It Done*	$24.95	$28.95	
	446	Learn to Listen	$24.95	$28.95	

Sales Tax

All purchases subject to applicable sales tax. Questions? Call **1-800-258-7248**

Subtotal	
Sales Tax (see note)	
Shipping and Handling ($1 one item; 50¢ each additional)	
Total	

Name _____ Title _____
Organization _____
Address _____ City _____
State/Province _____ZIP/Postal Code _____

Method of Payment
☐ Enclosed is my check or money order payable to National Seminars
☐ Please charge to: ☐ MasterCard ☐ Visa ☐ American Express
Signature _____Exp. Date _____
Card Number _____

Complete and send entire page by mail to:

IN U.S.A.:
National Press Publications
A Division of Rockhurst College
Continuing Education Center
6901 West 63rd Street • P.O. Box 2949 •
Shawnee Mission, KS 66201-1349

IN CANADA:
National Press Publications
A Division of Rockhurst College
Continuing Education Center
1243 Islington Avenue, Suite 900
Toronto, Ontario M8X 1Y9

Or call TOLL-FREE 1-800-258-7248 or FAX (913) 432-0824
VIP #705-008446-092